SESSIONS WITH EPHESIANS

Smyth & Helwys Publishing, Inc.
6316 Peake Road
Macon, Georgia 31210-3960
1-800-747-3016
© 2015 by William L. Self & Michael D. McCullar

Library of Congress Cataloging-in-Publication Data

Sessions with Ephesians : toward a new identity in Christ / by William Self and Michael McCullar.
pages cm
Includes bibliographical references.
ISBN 978-1-57312-838-4 (pbk. : alk. paper)
1. Bible. Ephesians--Commentaries. I. Title.
BS2695.53.S45 2015
227'.507--dc23

2015029763

Sessions *with*
Ephesians

● ● ●   Toward a *New*
            Identity in Christ

William L. Self & Michael D. McCullar

SMYTH&HELWYS
PUBLISHING, INCORPORATED · MACON, GEORGIA

Also by Michael McCullar

A Christian's Guide to Islam

Basics of Theology

Sessions with James

Sessions with Corinthians

Sessions with Timothy & Titus

James Annual Bible Study: Being Right in a Wrong World

Sessions with Mark
by Michael McCullar & Rickey Letson

Building Blocks for Sunday School Growth
by Bo Prosser with Michael McCullar & Charles Qualls

Also by William L. Self

Surviving the Stained Glass Jungle

Defining Moments:
First Lesson Sermons for Advent/Christmas/Epiphany

Survival Kit for the Stranded: Helps Those Who Hurt

The Saturday Night Special

Confessions of a Nomad: A Devotional Guide
by Carolyn Self & William L. Self

Before Thee I Wed by Bill & Carolyn Self

Survival Kit for Marriage by Carolyn Shealy Self and William L. Self

Bridging the Generation Gad by William L. Self

Learning to Pray by William L. Self & Carolyn Shealy Self

After Thee I Wed by William L. Self & Carolyn Shealy Self

This book is dedicated to the most loving, supportive church family in God's Kingdom. Johns Creek Baptist Church allowed us to lead, to equip and to exercise our gifts during years of relocation, re-creation, renewal, expansion and growth. Our church allowed each of us to utilize and apply our unique gifts to their fullest and supported us at every point on the collaborative journey. Our church also ministered to us and to our families and for this we are eternally grateful.

—Bill & Michael

Table of Contents

Introducing Ephesians

To read the Ephesian letter is to enter into a new realm of possibilities concerning God's plans for his people and his church. As Klyne Snodgrass writes, "Pound for pound Ephesians may be the most influential document ever written" (17). Paul's letter to the church in Ephesus opens the veil that has heretofore shrouded the purposes of God through the ages. In this letter we see where God wants to take the church, and, if we truly internalize its words, we see our own unique role in God's plans.

This letter is also timeless. John Mackay calls it "the most contemporary book in the Bible" (19). Strip it of just a few first-century references and it would be easily applicable to the modern church. It was, however, pointedly directed to the church of Paul's day that struggled with issues of inclusion and moving beyond the constraints of ancient Judaism. Large numbers of people became followers of Jesus after Pentecost, and though they were primarily Jews, they hailed from all over the Mediterranean basin. This led to a problem of assimilation that only grew worse as the gospel was preached successfully to the Gentiles. Large doses of disorder and subsequent chaos crept into the new churches as religious origins and cultures collided in the young faith communities.

Along with all of this came those who sought to commandeer the new communities for their own purposes. These voices brought their own insights and false doctrines into the Christian communities via philosophy-based teaching. The frenzy and confusion created by this influx of false instruction created the need for a unified theology, purpose, and direction. This would be true of any movement or organization that moves beyond its founding experience—thus the need for a document like the Ephesian letter.

The Ephesian letter was written approximately thirty-five years after the crucifixion of Jesus and is widely thought to have been authored by Paul. As is the case with most of Paul's work, there is some dispute as to whether he actually wrote the letter. In the end this is a futile exercise, as we have no way to determine definitive authorship, and if we did it wouldn't suddenly change how we interpret the words of the letter. It is indeed different in tenor and tone from most other Pauline works, but this difference could easily be attributed to the necessary subject matter inherent in the message. On the other hand, it is strikingly similar in some places to the letter to the Colossae church. This too can be easily dealt with when studying the similar issues facing both churches or, taken a step further, those faced by all contemporary churches of that era.

A succinct description of Ephesians would be as a letter in response to the issues of needing a definable doctrine and theological document to meet the needs of an expanding church that was literally being invaded by divisive and contrary philosophies. There was also a need to find a "rally point" for the church. The main church in Jerusalem was under extreme persecution and would fold under the pressure. The message and movement would spread, which is a good thing, but it would become so inclusive that age-old religious and cultural differences would emerge within small congregations, which is a bad thing. All believers and congregations would rally around one theme: Jesus. It sounds like a cliché taught at Vacation Bible School, but it is exactly what Paul believed the young churches needed most.

This letter would have been read through the lens of Jesus Christ as Lord so that the church in her calling as an organism and her conduct as an organization would be seen as Christo-centric. The doctrinal teaching of this epistle can be summed up by two words, "in Christ." Paul uses this term 167 times in his letters, signifying his deep belief that the mystical and holy relationship between Jesus and the church is the literal plan of God for eternity.

The Chosen Ones

Ephesians 1:3-14

In the original Greek, this passage is one long, complicated sentence. It is long and complicated because Paul is overwhelmed with praise for the God in Christ who has showered him with mercy and love by choosing him to serve the kingdom. The almost musical writing is reminiscent of one of the psalms. Paul's spirit is ecstatic. He has glimpsed the height and breadth and depth of God's activity and has seen God's love and grace up close. Paul, much like David, has seen both the beautiful and ugly sides of human existence. Once an enemy and persecutor of Jesus as Saul, he has been transformed into the righteous follower of Jesus renamed Paul. This restorative act alone is worthy of a life of praise, but Paul goes on to see God's transformative work each and every day in every walk of life.

Spiritual Blessings (1:3)

To say we are blessed is to make a grand understatement. We tend to toss that phrase around a great deal, but I doubt we stop long enough to give it the time it deserves. Paul tells us we are "blessed in the heavenly realms," which could mean a number of things, but none of them are plainly obvious. In fact, we have to continue reading the letter to fully grasp the full meaning of the statement. One thing is for certain, however: these blessings are given for the here and now and aren't reserved for our time with God after death. As Snodgrass writes, "In other words, 'heavenly realms' does not refer to a physical location but to a spiritual reality" (47). Far too many people have adopted a belief that blessings must be tangible. Ancient Hebrews believed that material blessings and health were signs of God's favor, and today we have the silly "Prosperity Gospel" that teaches we can demand material blessings (e.g., money) from God. Neither of these beliefs is germane to the New Testament. God does extend blessings in copious amounts, but these blessings originate from God and are entirely spiritual.

Chosen and Adopted (1:4-5)

The unusual sentence structure in verse 4 is similar to that of the Old Testament writings depicting God's choice of specific people for service. We might view God's plan for a person to accept salvation and God's choosing or calling that person for a specific life of ministry as being two distinctly different things. Paul would not. He finds that God is so personal and involved that God chooses each individual person for a life of sanctification and service. The beauty of God's choosing each person individually is twofold. First, Hebrews believed that God worked in a corporate way with Israel rather than approaching individuals. But Paul insists that God comes to each of us specifically. Second, God was at work in choosing us long before there was an "us." Hughes writes, "God's choosing antedated human need—indeed, human existence!" (23).

The talk of eternity and election in these verses can be confusing, but one thing is clear—God chose each of us for a definite purpose. Verse 4b tells us we are chosen to be both holy and blameless in the sight of God. We cannot be "out of the sight of God" no matter how hard we try (see Jonah). The takeaway from this portion of verse 4 is simple: our response to our calling is to be holy and blameless as much as it is humanly possible to be. Long before our creation, God planned for and provided for a life of dedicated, holy, and sacrificial living for each of us. As Barclay states, "Holy is the Greek word 'hagios,' which always has in it the idea of different and of separation. God is supremely holy because he is different from us. So, God chose Christians that they should be different from other people" (88). Holy is a state that we as individual believers must actively seek, but blameless is not something we can achieve. To be blameless is to be in a state of justification, a state of having our sins forgiven. And this is yet another beautiful element of God's long-term plans. God destined for each person to find forgiveness in Jesus and to live out that forgiveness as holy (different, separated) people. Again, long before there was a "me," God destined a future for me that included salvation and a life of purpose.

Verse 5 lays out how this is possible for Gentiles. In order for a Gentile to be added to God's family (remember Jews were the original chosen ones), an act of adoption has to take place. As an adoptive parent, I know well the hoops through which one has to jump in order to adopt a child. It takes a great deal of time, intention, patience, and often great expense to make an adoption happen, all of which God did for each of us. In the Greco-Roman world as in ours, adoption was a lengthy process that required much time and expense, and in the end the adoptive child was completely cut off from their former life while being given full legitimacy within his or her new family. It was as if the child died to the one family and was reborn to the new family. Again, this is simply too beautiful for words. Through Jesus, we Gentiles are adopted into God's family and are given full rights and privileges. And we have to symbolically die to the natural life we are born into before we are adopted into God's spiritual family in a process known as being born again!

Revealing a Mystery (1:9-10)

For the modern believer, none of what we read in Ephesians is "new" news, but for the early church that had only Judaism to draw from, it was groundbreaking material. Paul termed much of this message a mystery, but we must be careful here as our definition of mystery does not do justice to the meaning Paul had in mind: "In the New Testament a 'mystery' is something which has formerly been kept secret in the purposes of God but has now been disclosed" (Bruce, 261). Paul appears to see God's ultimate plan as if a veil has suddenly been lifted. It hasn't, obviously, as Paul is already privy to this reality after his encounter with Christ on the road to Damascus. In these verses, he is using a dramatic approach in order to teach the Ephesian believers proper theology about God's restorative plan for all people. As Wiersbe writes, "We are able to share in the secret that God will one day unite everything in Christ" (587). From the moment sin entered into the created order, the world has spiraled away from God's original plan. In other words, "Ever since sin came into the world, things have been falling apart" (Wiersbe, 587). The mystery Paul references is simply that God will pull the world back together and unite us all under Christ.

The Guarantee (1:13-14)

Christ is the person in whom God's uniting power is at work. Paul connects the sealing with the Holy Spirit to his remarks about Gentiles. All believers receive the Holy Spirit when they accept Christ, but the fact that Gentiles were sealed with the Spirit held a special significance with Paul. The Gentiles were not the original chosen people and were subsequently "one people removed" from God's original gift of salvation. Israel was to take God's saving grace to all other people groups, but for many reasons they erected barriers to keep God away rather than share their gift. In Jesus, and specifically through the Holy Spirit, Gentiles have a guarantee of God's grace and salvation. Barclay explains it this way: "In the ancient world when a sack, or a crate, or a package was dispatched, it was sealed with a seal, in order to indicate from where it had come and to whom it belonged. The possession of the Holy Spirit is the seal which shows that a person belongs to God" (100).

Paul is supplying irrefutable evidence that the Gentile Ephesians believers belong to God with the same certainty that Israel embodied over the centuries. "The Spirit is also a deposit on the future inheritance of believers" (Arnold, 93). Our inheritance is guaranteed, and what we enjoy today is but a glimpse of the magnitude of the glory that awaits.

Life Lessons

When the modern believer understands his or her place in God's plan for the world, it changes everything. God, through Jesus Christ and empowered by the Holy Spirit, is in the process of bringing all things together under the lordship of Christ. God chose for each of us to be part of the ongoing process of the restoration of creation. It is truly mind-boggling to comprehend, but we and the Ephesian Christians of two millennia ago are equal in God's plans. We share in the extravagance of God's grace and in the unique partnership we enjoy with God in bringing about his purposes.

God asks little of us in response to his acts of grace. He has provided the opportunity for us to be both blameless and holy so that we will align our mortal lives with his plans. To be holy is to be "different" and "separate" from the ungodliness of the natural world, and to be blameless means to have accepted spiritual justification through the salvation of Christ.

1. Were the Gentile Christians in Ephesus called and chosen to the same degrees and level that Israel was called? Explain your views.

_____

_____

_____

_____

_____

2. Contrast the similarities in the lives of David and Paul in relationship to God's restorative power.

_____

_____

_____

_____

_____

3. How do you grasp the idea that God chose us long before there was an "us"?

_____

_____

_____

_____

_____

4. Define the words _holy_ and _blameless_ in ways a modern believer could best understand.

_____

_____

_____

_____

_____

5. List things that Paul would say are involved in the "mystery of God." How would you describe this mystery in a sentence?

_____

_____

_____

_____

_____

6. Has Jesus already united everything according to God's purposes, or is this a future act? Explain your thoughts.

_____

_____

_____

_____

_____

7. What are the differences between our future inheritance and the spiritual blessings we are privy to in this life?

_____

_____

_____

_____

_____

8. List three ways that being "holy" and "blameless" can positively influence God's kingdom in today's world.

_____

_____

_____

_____

_____

Paul's Prayer for the Ephesian Believers

Ephesians 1:15-23

Paul's opening remarks (1:1-14) form a theology lesson of sorts for the Ephesian Gentile believers. He then shifts to a liturgy of praise, prayer, and encouragement for the progress they have made over the years since his last visit. Make no mistake: Paul is still in full teaching mode, but he is doing so while also in a posture of praise and prayer. Peter T. O'Brien describes it this way: "The paragraph as a whole with its long sentence containing a thanksgiving (vv. 15-16a), an intercession (vv. 16b-19), and confessional material in praise of God who has raised and exalted Christ (vv. 20-23), presents God's purposes for his people on a broad canvas" (126). Paul is driving home the reality that everything God has thus far done has been for his people, which includes the Gentile Ephesians. "Clearly the apostle wants his readers to appropriate more fully 'every spiritual blessing' that has graciously been given to them in Christ" (O'Brien, 126).

Paul Prays (1:15-16)

Paul is in prison when he writes this epistle to the church in Ephesus. To say he has time on his hands is a grand understatement, but to realize the extent and scope of his prayer practices is to be amazed. When the reports come to him about the state of the church in Ephesus, he immediately enters a prolonged period of prayer focused on the church and the congregants. Paul likely feels a proper level of pride about the increasing maturity of the formerly pagan Ephesians, many of whom he knows from his earlier visit. Much like Paul, the Ephesian believers persevere and grow in their faith despite increasing and pervasive persecution. Paul is in prison and the Ephesians are being hammered by Hebrew purists, yet both are progressing, maturing, and making a profound difference.

Wisdom and Understanding (1:17-18)

The opening portion of Paul's prayer seeks supernatural wisdom and revelation so that the Ephesians will know Jesus in more and deeper ways. It is a given that they are intimate with God and maturing as a faith community, but Paul is affirming the faith fact that spiritual maturing is an unending process and pursuit. As a believer matures, she taps into the ever-increasing power of the Holy Spirit for wisdom that allows for a deeper understanding of the things of God. This is a series of benefits for any believer, yet one that unmotivated, static Christians never realize.

The Greek word for wisdom is *Sophia*, which holds a connotation of "deeper understanding." While the word was commonly used in the Greco-Roman world, especially by Greek philosophers and teachers, it is a particularly appropriate part of Paul's petition. The average Gentile Ephesian believer would have come from a lively pagan background that included many gods, goddesses, demons, and spirits. It would have been important to continue to stress the reality of one God and the supreme power held by God. Barclay writes, "In Paul's day, people strongly believed both in demons and angels; and these words which Paul uses are the titles of different grades of angels. He is saying that there is not a being in heaven or on earth to whom Jesus Christ is not superior" (105).

The first-century world of Ephesus would have featured a deep-seated belief in fate as the prime determinant of life. The belief that the flow of life was effectively left up to the fickle "fates" led to a pervasive anxiety and resignation that followers of Jesus not only had to counter but also had to personally battle and resist. Arnold quotes the first-century Stoic writer Manilius:

> Set your minds free, mortal men, let your cares go and deliver your lives from all this pointless fuss. Fate rules the world; everything is bound by certain laws; eternities are sealed by predetermined events . . . . No one can catch her if she comes close to him. Everyone must bear his appointed lot. (108)

The notion that fate is the end-all determining factor in life's events is all but alien to our culture, but it was *the* prevailing belief in Ephesus. We realize that living in the created natural world brings inherent risks on a daily basis. We believe God can play the prime role in who and what we become and what we do with our lives. To give any of this to blind fate would be to opt for a fatalistic mindset.

Paul's use of inheritance in verse 18c is easily and often misinterpreted. Much like in the Exodus rendering, this usage of inheritance is focused more on God than on individual people of faith. A modern believer might easily jump to a future-view focus relating to an inheritance in the afterlife. It's a "when we all get to heaven" mentality. But Paul is saying that we are God's inheritance, not the other way around. Much like in the Old Testament exodus story, Jesus has become the redemption that has freed God's people and, in the process, become the symbol of God's new inheritance. This is truly sobering if we consider the massive responsibility involved as *we* the people of God must live up to and live out our calling as God's inheritance. This is a mantle to wear that brings with it great honor and great responsibility.

God's Power (1:19-20)

The Ephesians lived in an era when true, tangible power was believed to be vested in the multiple gods and goddesses and in the Roman Empire. The average person would have felt powerless in contrast to the mythical might of Diana or Herakles, and completely at the mercy of Rome. Paul would not disagree for one comprehensive reason: the power of which he speaks is supernatural and eternal rather than brutish and in real time. The mythical Greek gods did not actually exist, but this was not yet an acceptable idea; thus they were both feared and revered. Rome was all powerful and would have continued dominance for three hundred years. Despite both of these realities, Paul teaches of God being stronger, more powerful, and, to raise the stakes, everlasting in contrast to the temporary might of the Greco-Roman world. The Roman Empire lasted for fewer than five hundred years, which is an amazingly long time for humans but a blip on the screen in light of eternity.

Paul uses the example of the greatest exhibition of power ever recorded when he cites the resurrection of Jesus from the dead. The Greek word favored by Paul for power is *Dunamis*, which is the root of the English word *dynamite*. Paul uses it more than one hundred times in his letters to denote the immense strength and power held by God. Paul is telling the Ephesian believers that the very same power God tapped to defeat death and sin in the resurrection is available to them as individual followers of Christ. Hughes depicts God's exertion of power this way:

> The greatest display of this power was seen "when God raised Christ from the dead." Just as the cross is the highest display of God's love, so the resurrection is the ultimate display of his power. No created force could ever do this! But what Paul wants us to see personally and practically is that "his incomparably great power is for us who believe." (58).

Arnold states that Paul's central concern in his prayer is for the Holy Spirit to expand their awareness of God's power available to them (121). This would have come as both revelation and shock to the Ephesian Christians and would take a good bit of unpacking for them to fully comprehend. Paul uses a sequential approach in explaining that Christ:

> Was raised from the dead and is seated at the right hand in the heavenly realm.
> Is high above every principality and power, might and domain, and every name named, not only in this present age but also in the coming age.
> All things are subjected to him.

It took the Ephesian believers time, but they began to grasp the differences between spiritual power and the power exerted by Rome and the Hebrew purists. This theological breakthrough broadened their concept of both God the Father and God the Son and their combined lordship over all things created, whether earthly or found in the heavenly realm (v. 21). Jesus was placed primary over all things and all realms with a name that is above all names. Jesus is the true *end-all*.

Life Lessons

Paul presents a theology that is uniquely complicated. In a play on the words of Plato, William Barclay states, "The unexamined religion is the religion not worth having. It is an obligation for thinking people to think their way to God" (104). In essence this is exactly what Paul is urging the Ephesian believers to do as they think on the issues of God's provisional wisdom, the inherent power God gives his children, how that power was exhibited in the death and resurrection of Jesus, and how Jesus has been given dominion over all things, especially the church. He is teaching primary theology to Christians who have only pagan backgrounds to draw from. He is alerting people to the amazing amount of power available to them through the Holy Spirit, even though the Holy Spirit is a difficult concept for them to grasp. And he is telling them that fate is a farce, even though fate was the life-defining focus of their previous lives.

Paul's "theology dump" was a lot for his original readers to absorb in such short order. Truth be told, it's a lot for us to deal with as well. Paul's teaching, however, is pivotal to the totality of Christian theology and practice. What the Ephesians needed to grasp and employ is exactly what we as modern believers need to grasp and employ. At a minimum, we must realize how much we matter to God and to God's kingdom plans. God worked in Christ and is now at work in us so that we may be at work for him. Steve Motyer writes, "With the greatest reverence, but with fantastic boldness, Paul describes the church as *that which completes* Christ" (48). Christ is in the process of completing us, and we have been given the privilege to, in the words of Motyer, "complete Christ." Christ is using the church universal to complete God's plans for creation. This is a concise statement that sums up our theology and our life's calling.

1. What can Paul's long opening prayer teach us about our personal prayer lives?

_____

_____

_____

_____

_____

2. Is there a difference between tangible and actual material blessings and the spiritual blessings Paul speaks of?

_____

_____

_____

_____

_____

3. What are attributes of a progressive, incremental spiritual maturity in a believer's life?

_____

_____

_____

_____

_____

4. True or false: People today continue to believe in demons and spirits.

_____

_____

_____

_____

_____

5. Does fate continue to figure into the way people view life in today's modern, intellectual world? Explain your views.

_____

_____

_____

_____

_____

6. Paul teaches that we are provided the same power in our lives that was evident in Jesus' life. List ways we can utilize this power and the possible outcomes.

_____

_____

_____

_____

_____

7. "Christ is exalted above every conceivable intelligence—angelic, demonic or human" (Hughes, 60). If Jesus is truly above all things and has ultimate power, why is the world filled with so much evil?

_____

_____

_____

_____

_____

The Way We Were

Ephesians 2:1-10

In chapter 1, Paul prayed that the Ephesian Christians would be open to a deeper appreciation of God's immense power that was shown in the resurrection of Jesus from the dead. The entire chapter was devoted to an exposition of God's ultimate power and plan through Christ and for the church. In chapter 2, he shifts to a focus on personal responsibility for the sin condition each person inherits by birth. It is likely that Paul is teaching in a more technical way what the Ephesian church has already experienced but are having trouble explaining. If it is a correct assumption that all Christians should know what they believe, why they believe as they do, and are capable of being conversational about it, then Paul's teaching is essential and timeless.

Paul focuses on two basic themes in the second chapter of his letter. He deals with redemption and forgiveness and applies each to the reconciliation of our sinful base nature, later adding the theme of unity to the mix. Any and all unity is contingent on our sin conditions being justified and thus reconciled through Jesus. To this end, Paul describes "the horrible condition humanity faces: death, slavery and condemnation" (Arnold, 312). Paul deals with the "lost" condition of any person (Jew or Gentile) who is outside of a faith relationship with Christ. He doesn't say that they are "sick" or "damaged"; he says they are "dead." No doubt he has their attention and is able to instruct the Ephesians on the perils of going it alone in life.

The Birth *Effect* (2:1-3)

Paul begins with a graphic description of the damaged material with which God has to work. "You" is a shortening of "You Gentiles," in contrast to "We also," meaning Jews. This makes sense when placed next to Paul's earlier teaching about Gentiles being adopted into God's family and Israel's status as the original chosen people. Paul is saying that all people, regardless of religious or ethnic origin, share the same birth *effect* of sin and are dead spiritually outside of a faith relationship with Jesus. The "before-Christ" state is Paul's jumping-off point in explaining that without the saving grace provided by Jesus, all people are spiritually dead. O'Brien points to an environment of evil (the ways of this world, v. 2), an inner inclination towards evil (the cravings of our sinful nature, v. 3), and a supernaturally powerful opponent (the ruler of the Kingdom of the Air, the spirit who is now at work in those who are disobedient, v. 2) (155–56).

Wiersbe speaks of a person being spiritually dead, unable to understand or appreciate spiritual things, just as a physically dead person is incapable of responding to any stimuli (591). While many things can lead to a physical death, Paul stipulates that unresolved sin leads to spiritual death. In Romans 6:23 Paul plainly states, "The wages of sin is death." Phillips writes, "We were not just dead; we were dead in trespasses. The Greek word translated *trespasses* is *paratoma*, which means 'a falling aside when one should have stood upright'" (59). This is the same word utilized in depicting the fall of Adam and Eve. Its companion word describes sin as missing the mark in the way an archer might aim an arrow but miss the target.

Paul uses *hamartia* to define sin and *sarx* to define a person's natural sinful nature. He describes a person who willfully walks in a way of life that leaves God out of the equation. This is depicted as an intentional choice that is alien to "walking in good works in accordance with God's design" (Arnold, 126). In order for us to have the relationship with God that Christ allows for, we must overcome our "transgressions and sin." To do so successfully requires each person to realize and admit the problems, and then to seek restoration.

PROBLEM #1

Paul cites the first problem as "the ways of this world" (v. 2). There is more than one way these words can be defined, as Gentiles and Jews might read different meanings into them, but the easiest way is simply to see them as referring to the age in which they lived. O'Brien suggests that Paul is speaking about the spatial and temporal aspects of fallen human existence (159). Wiersbe sees it as "a world system that puts pressure on each person to try to get them to conform" (592). Bruce opts for "the present age that is dominated by the forces of evil" (280), and Hughes says, "The word translated 'world' (*Kosmos*) is used 186 times in the Greek New Testament, and virtually every instance has evil connotations" (66). The Ephesians are contemplating the inherently evil age in which they live, one that by its nature works against God and their salvation.

PROBLEM #2

The second problem faced by the Ephesian believers is "the ruler of the kingdom of the air" (v. 2). Ephesians contains more references to principalities and powers than any other letter in the New Testament. Paul is saying that the ultimate authority and power is Satan, often termed the "ruler of the kingdom of the air." In that era, it was believed that the realm of the air was the space between heaven and earth, a virtual *no-man's land* inhabited by evil spirits. The lead evil spirit is the devil, who seeks to make people "children of disobedience." This is a genuine issue for Christians, as there is a force working against them when they seek to live righteously.

PROBLEM #3

The third issue Paul cites is "the cravings of our sinful nature" (v. 3). The Christian has been justified, forgiven, and redeemed, but he or she continues to grapple with sin. There is the ever-present evil age to deal with as well as a living personification of evil to fend off, but the *coup de grace* for most believers seems to be the former sinful nature that seems to constantly nudge us the wrong way. Despite being a "new person in Christ," we daily battle the former, old person mired in sin. The ancient Jewish theology contained a notion that every person struggled with an inner propensity toward evil; it was called the evil impulse (Arnold, 313).

This array of evil forces combined with the tendency to become "objects of wrath" (v. 3) creates a regular opportunity to move away from God. There is, as Arnold states, "a compelling pull on people to sin and transgress God's commandments. People need deliverance and freedom from the overwhelming power of these forces" (313).

Saving Grace (2:4-10)

After laying out the complexities of the inherent sin condition of the Ephesian believers, Paul concisely presents the remedy: "But because of his great love for us, God, who is rich in mercy, made us alive with

Christ even when we were dead in transgressions—it is by grace you have been saved" (vv. 4-5). Verse 4 is the hinge on which this whole section turns. Paul has written graphically of the human condition and our utter inability to solve it. Now he introduces the only answer to the human sin condition with the words *But God* . . . .

> In light of the distressing plight humanity faces because of the powerful chains of their slavery, the "but God" of this paragraph shines a brilliant ray of hope. The God of creation is not only just, but he is merciful—exceedingly so. The introductory blessing has already characterized God as rich in grace (1:7). But God is also rich in mercy. (Arnold, 134)

It is important to note who is making these bold claims on behalf of God. This is Paul, who as Saul was a great persecutor of the Christian movement. Paul was party to the killing of Stephen, and his agenda was to rid the land of those who believed Jesus to be the Messiah. Saul was not a person of grace or mercy, yet after his conversion he became the leading evangelist for the God of grace and mercy. Paul not only believes these words; he is a product of them. As Paul writes to Titus, "he saved us, not because of righteous things we had done, but because of his mercy" (Titus 3:5).

The use of *charis* would not have been familiar to Gentiles, but the Hebrews had used it to describe God's love for centuries. This is the word most often used to describe God's grace in the New Testament and was personified in the life, sacrifice, and resurrection of Jesus. The concept of New Testament grace also carries the connotation of being totally and completely undeserved. Verse 5 strikes the line between a gift and a deed. The natural thought would include the necessity of earning favor as humans seem to be wired to work toward rewards. Paul cautions, however, that salvation is by faith alone, as it could not possibly be earned by anyone. The heavy lifting has already been done by God the Father and God the Son on the cross and in the resurrection. The "work" is finished, leaving only a faith-based acceptance to bring salvation.

You Lucky Gentiles (2:11-22)

Paul shifts his focus to the reality that there are two basic people groups within the framework of God's creation. God created Israel to be a nation of priests and a holy nation with a calling to reconcile the world back to him. Wiersbe writes, "God called the Jews, beginning with Abraham, that through them he might reveal himself as the one true God. With the Jews he deposited his Word, and through the Jews he gave the world the Savior" (595). Obviously the Jews are pivotal in God's reconciliation strategies for all humankind.

The non-Jews, or Gentiles, however, are outside any covenant relationships with God, and in the words of Paul, they are "excluded from citizenship in Israel . . . without hope and without God in the world" (v. 12). *Wow, thanks for the pep talk, Paul!* Paul isn't disrespecting the Gentile Ephesians; rather he is demonstrating the change brought about by the actions of Jesus. A wedge had been driven between Jews and Gentiles via traditions, how the Law was being interpreted, and the all but completely exclusive nature of Israel. Most Greco-Roman Gentiles were religious but had chased after the entire pantheon of gods and goddesses for so long that their belief system was both convoluted and fruitless. Paul is simply speaking the obvious truths of the state of the Gentiles in Ephesus, one of the most pagan cities of antiquity.

Paul next reminds them of how Jesus spanned the gap and literally became the bridge so that the Gentiles can be part of God's plans. He refers to the barriers between the Jews and Gentiles as "the wall of hostility" (v. 14) and is alluding to the actual barrier that existed inside the temple structure. Gentiles were allowed to enter the outer areas of the temple complex but were restricted beyond a certain point by a large, long four-and-a-half-foot wall that surrounded the inner courts.

> The Jewish historian Josephus informs us that thirteen stone slabs written in Greek and Latin stood at intervals on the barrier warning Gentiles not to enter. Inscribed on the stones were these words: *No foreigner is to enter within the forecourt and the balestrade around the sanctuary. Whoever is caught will have himself to blame for his subsequent death.* (Arnold, 316–17)

The exclusivity of the Jews is apparent within the temple, which was simply a microcosm of the huge divisions in place that seemed to have no natural solution. It took a supernatural, provisional act of God to dismantle the multiple obstructions that would provide access to God from all directions. Jesus instituted this shift that was still unfolding twenty-plus years later in Ephesus.

Verses 19-22 form a second Magna Carta of the faith (the first being Galatians 3:28-29) that unites all the peoples of creation as one people, the people of God. Jesus had erased the ethnic, religious, cultural, and gender divisions that had plagued and derailed God's plans for humanity. This would also become a time when God would leave the temple and find his dwelling place within each believer. The temple had been the center of faith for thousands of years but was replaced by the resurrected Jesus and the arrival of God's Spirit. This teaching would become even more important a few years later upon the destruction of the temple in the ill-advised Jewish war on Roman forces in Jerusalem. Barclay sums it up expertly: "This is what the church should be like. Its unity comes not from organization, or ritual, or liturgy; it comes from Christ. *Ubi Christus, ibi ecclesia*—Where Christ is, there is the Church" (137).

Life Lessons

John the Baptist preached a call to personal repentance. Jesus taught and exampled a personal relationship with God that would provide salvation and a life of spiritual direction. The early church struggled with the scope of both due to the personal and theological conflicts they encountered within Judaism. To be saved by grace rather than through God's provisions with Israel was so revolutionary and so counter to tradition that the distance between Jew and Christian grew exponentially. God's love and provisions for grace grew as well, however, as it expanded to cover all people.

The best person to promote God's massively expansive grace was Paul, as he had lived and led from both sides. Paul was a living testament to God's grace and to the subsequent persecution of Satan as he worked out his salvation daily. Our takeaway? We too are products of God's grace, and we also face the daily temptation to re-embrace our former "dead" lives. The "way we were" is no longer our permanent state. The "way we are now" is God's plan for our lives. To reject our former selves is our daily cross to bear. Paul urged the Ephesian church to follow his lead and example. We have the privilege of doing so today as well.

1. Why is it important for believers to know what they believe, to recognize why they believe as they do, and to be able to be conversational about their faith?

_____

_____

_____

_____

_____

2. Describe Paul's depiction of a person who is spiritually dead.

_____

_____

_____

_____

_____

3. What are the differences between the Hebrew salvation process and that of Christianity?

_____

_____

_____

_____

_____

4. How does Paul describe the work of Satan to the Ephesian readers?

_____

_____

_____

_____

_____

5. What are possible reasons Christians tend to drop back and re-adopt sinful practices of their former lives?

_____

_____

_____

_____

_____

6. Describe the differences between Saul the Jewish traditionalist and Paul the redeemed follower of Christ. Craft a definition of grace from your descriptions.

_____

_____

_____

_____

_____

7. Why do you think Jews did not allow Gentiles into the innermost portions of the temple?

_____

_____

_____

_____

_____

8. If the Latin phrase *Ubi Christus, ibi ecclesia* (Where Christ is, there is the Church) is correct, is the church as we know it necessary? Elaborate on your views.

_____

_____

_____

_____

_____

A Letter from the Roman Jail

Ephesians 3:1-21

Have you ever wondered if Paul's on-again, off-again status as an inmate of the Roman Prison Authority diluted his authority and subsequent message? Surely a malcontent or Hebrew purist reminded the Ephesian church that Paul was yet again serving time in the clink and, as a repeat offender, should not be trusted in matters of great importance. This may be one of the reasons Paul so regularly uses the first person pronoun "I" in his letters followed by "a prisoner." Any public relations guru would recommend being up front about the jail time in an effort to get out ahead of the issue. In today's image-obsessed climate, people often hear the advice, "One must control the conversation." Paul, however, was not the average convict. In proper context, Paul was in the custody of Nero. He had violated the sanctity of the temple by taking a Gentile beyond the proper and posted boundaries. He also had the audacity to proclaim that Jews and Gentiles were equal before God. *Is there no end to this man's crimes?*

When Paul calls himself a "prisoner of Christ Jesus for the sake of you Gentiles," he is boldly citing his incarceration and linking it with his service to God's unfolding plans. Paul's incarceration (and later death) is consistent with those who served God with devotion and boldness in both the Old and New Testaments despite enduring persecution and often a martyr's death. For Paul, being in prison was further confirmation of the reality of his true calling as God's vehicle for reaching the Gentiles.

Defining Paul (3:1-2)

Dale Moody summed up Paul's ministry in this concise way: "Paul is to accomplish God's purposes among the Gentiles as Peter was assigned the mission to the Jews" (65). Arnold adds, "God has revealed a new and definitive stage in his eternal plan that involves creating a people for himself consisting of the Jews and Gentiles united to Christ and joined together. All who have faith in Christ Jesus become a part of this new community and have direct access to the Father" (180). Paul sees himself as being divinely called to preach and teach this new arrangement, which he deems a mystery, ushering in a new age for all humankind. For today's Christian, this new arrangement is neither new nor novel as it is all we have ever known. From the second century forward, Christianity has been dominated by Gentiles as the Jewish wing of the movement waned after the Hebrew revolt of the early 70s AD. The dramatic coming together of Jew and Gentile was a seismic shift for the Eastern world in the mid-first century, although the years have desensitized today's church to its import. Then, however, it was such a contentious issue that many people died bringing it into reality.

Interpreters have commented on the radical nature of Paul's mission:

> The only reason Paul was in prison was because he thought Gentiles had the same access to God Jews did. If he had been content to be a Jewish Christian with a mission to Jews or if he had been willing to help Gentiles on a lower plain, he would not have been in jail. (Snodgrass, 159)

> The Jews were infuriated when Paul taught that believing Gentiles were full members of God's family. The Jews' national pride was stung. Even in the church many Jewish believers thought that Gentiles should become Jews in order to be Christians, or at least they should be regarded as second-class citizens in the Kingdom. (Phillips, 79)

Paul obviously disagrees and thus makes it his new life's calling to reach out to Gentiles with the inclusive gospel of Christ. He seems to consider being in prison both an honor and a hindrance. His imprisonment does not allow for him to travel and teach, but it is for the noblest of causes. This is accentuated by his statement that he is not a prisoner of Rome but a prisoner *for* Christ. He truly feels that the only reason Nero has any power over him is due to God's allowance. His imprisonment is simply *part of the drill of being Paul.* That said, he does have a mystery to share and wants the prison gig to end soon.

The Origin of the Mystery (3:3-6)

Paul's ministry and mission could be defined as simply being "the bearer and proclaimer of God's mystery." Again, for modern readers, there is no mystery left as two thousand years of including Gentiles has made this more the norm than the exception. For the Gentile in Ephesus during the mid-first century, though, this was indeed new news that needed a great deal of explanation. "In the New Testament, a *mystery* is not eerie or inscrutable, but rather 'a truth that was hidden by God in times past and is now revealed to those who are in His family.' A *mystery* is a 'sacred secret' that is unknown to unbelievers but understood and treasured by the people of God" (Wiersbe, 598). I must take exception with Dr. Wiersbe at this point, as not all people of God were treasuring this unfolding mystery. Paul's main obstacle was Christian Jews who continued to draw lines of demarcation between themselves and Gentiles who believed in Jesus as Lord. Since this sacred secret was one of progressive revelation and was not stated outright in the Old Testament, the Hebrew believers in Christ were heaping additional requirements on Gentiles who found God through Jesus.

Possibly the most difficult aspect of God's mystery is that of unity. Unity is an ideal that is easier to laud than to live, and sadly little has changed in the two millennia since Paul penned these words. Unity is undoubtedly, however, Paul's meaning in verse 6 as he literally "coined a word in order to describe the intimate relation that Jews and Gentiles have to each other in the body of Christ" (Patzia, 212). J. A. Robinson ups the ante on this concept: "There is no English equivalent and, in order to capture its full meaning it would read this way; In relation to the Body the members are 'incorporate,' in relation to one another they are 'concorporate;' that is sharers in the one body" (78).

If the truth were told, the largest issue at play in Ephesus and in other first-century Christian churches would not be solving the mystery. It would be accepting the other party. Jews didn't care for Gentiles, and after centuries of enmity and exclusion Gentiles felt no love for Hebrews. Unraveling the "mystery" was not as problematic as applying the contents of that mystery. This reality was not new to first-century Ephesus. People groups have disliked one another since the beginning of recorded history, and this reality continues to play out today.

The gospel, however, made internal battles unnecessary and even more counterproductive than ever before. Not accepting a person of another ethnic or religious group due solely to their difference is denying the potential reality of the gospel in his or her life. Plus, we must see God's still-unfolding mystery as bigger than any of us. As Patzia states, "Earlier, the author indicated that God's ultimate plan was to bring all creation together (1:10). One gets the distinct impression that the unity between Jew and Gentile is but the first step in a broader cosmic unity that is going to include all of creation under the Lordship of Christ (cf. Rom. 8:19-21)" (212). J. B. Phillips offer this succinct and to-the-point theological truth: "Love toward God does not exist without love to fellow humanity" (78).

The Stewardship of Paul (3:7-13)

Earlier Paul referred to his role as a "steward" and in some translations as an "administrator" of God's mystery. He also saw himself as a true apostle, even though that title was reserved for those who were with Jesus during his earthly ministry. Paul likened his Damascus Road encounter with the risen Christ to having spent time with Jesus; thus, the experience gave him genuine claim to the title of apostle. If there were a vote on this matter, I'd cast a *yay* for Paul's claim. Being struck down and then blinded by encountering the risen Christ is the stuff of apostles!

Life Lessons

The word "mystery" has shifted in practical meaning over the years since Paul wrote this letter. A modern person would see a mystery as being solvable if the correct amount of reason and deduction were applied. To the person living in the mid-first century, a mystery would be a hidden reality that only the wisest of the wise or a god or goddess could clarify and solve. This is closer to Paul's usage as he speaks to God's great mystery that began to be revealed in Christ. People groups have sparred since the beginning of time. Jews looked down on Gentiles, the Gentiles felt the same about the Jews, and the Samaritans were seen as below second class by the Jews. Since these distinctions covered everyone alive at that point, it's easy to see how much enmity existed between people groups. Add religions into the mix, and it becomes even more problematic. The mystery Paul taught was God's ultimate plan of bringing all of creation under the lordship of Christ. Paul's message infuriated the Jews who had chosen to not trust Jesus as the long-awaited Messiah. *Gentiles equal to Jews in all ways? No way!*

The traditional Jews didn't accept the message of Paul and chose to remain outside God's new inclusive, unified framework. Paul's message would, in the end, lead to his death. We can *tsk-tsk* the fundamentalist Jews, but we shouldn't. Instead, we should ask ourselves if we have similar animosity for people unlike us. Have we continued the behind-the-scenes bigotry by simply shifting the people groups around? Are modern Christians as exclusive as first-century Jews? These are questions we must ask. God's mystery continues to unfold, and we are called to make it available to all people. As Paul was a "steward of the mystery," so must we be also.

1. The early church faced disunity between traditional Hebrews and Gentile Christians. This interpersonal and group dissension hampered the progress of God's work. What factors lead to disunity in the modern church?

_____

_____

_____

_____

_____

2. If it is true that the coming together of Jew and Gentile was the first step in a broader plan for unity, what still remains to be unified today? Will there ever be genuine unity?

_____

_____

_____

_____

_____

3. Paul stated that he was a prisoner of Jesus Christ, yet he was actually a prisoner of Nero and Rome. What did he mean with his statement of being a prisoner of Jesus?

_____

_____

_____

_____

_____

4. How would you define the "mystery" Paul speaks about so often throughout this letter?

_____

_____

_____

_____

5. Were there issues of disunity between Gentile and Jewish Christians? In what ways did each group live out their faith uniquely?

_____

_____

_____

_____

_____

6. Paul deemed himself an apostle even though he wasn't with Jesus during his earthly ministry. Why did he view himself as an apostle? Did this label help or hinder his ministry?

_____

_____

_____

_____

_____

7. What do you think of Patzia's idea of believers being both "incorporate" and "concorporate"?

_____

_____

_____

_____

_____

8. J. B. Phillips wrote, "Love toward God does not exist without love to fellow humanity." Assuming he is correct, can we say we truly love God? Elaborate on your answer.

_____

_____

_____

_____

_____

Thou Shalt Not Misbehave

Ephesians 4:1-6

Session **5**

Ephesians features perhaps the smoothest transition of all twenty-seven letters of the New Testament. Over the first three chapters the theological groundwork is laid for a unified people serving the one God. Everything about the new expression of faith was based on unity:

• One Faith
• One God
• One Messiah
• One Message
• One People

This intense theological and doctrinal focus on unity was necessary due to the increasing estrangement of relationships with Judaism, especially the wealthy and well-positioned Jewish elite. Another reason for Paul's focus was the amount of inferior and false teaching from Gnostics and other non-Christian teachers and philosophies that infiltrated the newly established churches. These were formative years for the church, and the stability of the new congregations was of paramount importance to the movement. Add to this the reality that most new believers were spiritual novices, and the stakes grow exponentially. A basic foundational theological groundwork had to be laid if the Ephesian church, and many others like it, was to make it to the turn of the second century.

Beginning in chapter 4, Paul essentially states that even the best theology is nothing more than lofty, well-intentioned words without actual application in one's life. To this end he builds on the prior theological teaching with an almost James-like instruction in basic faith living. The final three chapters are plain, simple, and easily applicable teachings on how to live a life of faith based on the examples and teachings of Jesus. One can also see Paul urging the Ephesus church to see the need to live *up* to the high calling associated with being a follower of Jesus. Illustrative of this is a story told by Bruce Bickel and Stan Jantz in *Ephesians: Finding Your Identity in Christ:*

> There's an old story about the world conqueror Alexander the Great. The mythic Macedonian was inspecting his troops when he came upon a shabbily dressed soldier. "What's your name?" the great military genius asked. "Alexander," the soldier replied. Without missing a beat, Alexander the Commander took a step forward and said to the now trembling infantryman, "Either change your ways or change your name." (96)

The message is clear: Christians are identified with Jesus and as such must constantly and with vigilance seek to best exemplify him through conduct in all areas. The secondary message is equally important: we literally owe God our best due to the enormous gifts of salvation, peace, purpose, and a course to follow in life. R. Kent Hughes sums it up this way:

> Paul urges the Ephesians (and us) "to live a life worthy of the calling you have received." The Greek word translated "worthy" is "axios," which has the root idea of weight. This is the word from which we derive our English word "axiom," which means, "to be of equal weight." In an equation the axiom indicates doing something to each side of the equation so it remains true. Paul is saying we should try to live lives equal to the great blessings described in chapters 1 through 3. We are to be like the man who said, "Christ has done so much for me, the rest of my life is a P.S. to his great work!" (121)

Klyne Snodgrass adds,

> Throughout the New Testament, ethical imperatives are based on theological indicatives. Obedience is always a response to grace. God acts first, and humans respond. . . . If God's love is so great, if his salvation is so powerful, if God has granted such reconciliation, then believers should live accordingly. They should value God's love enough to be shaped by it. Note that "calling" is used for salvation and responsibility of every Christian, not of the

"professional ministry" or an elite group. This one call is for all Christians to live in accord with what God has done. (194, 196)

Being Worth Your Salt (4:1-6)

In the time of the Roman world, dominance soldiers were often paid with salt. Salt was pivotal in preserving and seasoning food and was scarce. This made it a premium. Any early Christian would recognize the phrase "being worth your salt." Paul didn't use this term in describing the Christian's unique responsibilities to God. He played the "prison" card and told them, "you must live up to the calling you have received" (4:1). Paul likely saw his prison time as the cost for visibly living out his faith. His service and allegiance to Jesus cost him his freedom and later his life. In the inverse, counterintuitive world of Jesus, the loss of freedom and the ignominy of prison would have been Paul merely living up to the high calling of Christ. Remember, in Christ "the first shall be last and the last shall be first." This calling is not of this world and certainly not of the social orders of the past two thousand years.

BE HUMBLE (4:2)

Humility was not a virtue in either the Greek or Roman cultures. It was seen as a cardinal weakness that bordered on exhibiting a lack of respect for one's self. A "real man" would never be humble lest he be seen as weak, easy to defeat or swindle. Hebrews were taught humility throughout the Old Testament, and God called them to use this as a way to highlight their differences. Paul was not writing to a predominantly Hebrew-Christian group in this letter, however; he was writing to Gentiles who had been steeped in the Greco-Roman ideologies that humility was for weaklings. For them, blatant humility could get you killed.

Today's world (both the East and the West) also tends to see humility as a possible liability. This suggests that genuine humility is not a natural trait in the average person and that our societies continue to undervalue it. To be humble is to act out "agape" love: placing the needs of other people ahead of our own. To live up to our calling in Christ is to exhibit the life-character traits that Jesus exampled. They were completely countercultural and indicative of counter-organized religion. This is especially true of humility, as this one trait was instrumental in the death of Jesus. He gave his life for humankind. No one took his life. He willingly gave it up. This is the true definition of humility. If we follow Jesus' example, we must also work against our natural inclinations of pride and seeking advantage. Humility is one virtue that can demonstrate our unique difference as Christians.

Be Gentle (4:2)

Webster's Dictionary defines gentleness as "being mild in manner or effect" (116). The King James Version of the New Testament substitutes "meekness" for gentleness, but in reality neither adequately does justice to the complex Greek word Paul used. Possibly the best option would be to use Aristotle's unique practice of defining all virtues as the midpoint between two extremes. William Barclay quotes Aristotle as defining the Greek word in question as "the midpoint between getting too angry and never being angry at all" (158). Another ancient Greek idea would be the Golden Mean. Biblical gentleness would be the absence of both anger problems and complete apathy. As Christians, there are things we should become upset about; there is no arguing that Jesus was demonstrably angry when clearing the temple. Conversely, we must not see our faith as needing to be held in check to the point of pure apathy. There are no lauded examples in the New Testament of disciples who sat on their hands while they awaited the return of Christ. It might be a good thing for churches to hang a sign over the entry doors reading "No Apathy Allowed!"

This midpoint would be a level of living that demonstrates agape-love and provides an example of how to best treat other people. Gentleness is a proactive lifestyle that seeks to touch others with the kindness and humility that we seek for our own lives. In essence, we wish for others to see something in us that they would love to have for themselves.

Be Patient (4:2)

I've heard it said that the true test of patience is the time it takes an elevator door to close after the choice of floor is made. If that's a true indication of how impatient we are as a people, we have a long way to go to reach the standard Paul is teaching. Patience essentially means the ability to wait. Bickel and Jantz add, "When you are characterized by patience, you are willing to wait on the Lord for His timing. You are willing to wait for other people whose personalities annoy you. And you are willing to wait for God's answers when you are experiencing difficulties" (98). Plus, you'll be much more spiritual in elevators!

Bear One Another in Love (4:2)

John R. W. Stott defines this "forbearing" as "that mutual tolerance without which no group of human beings can live together" (149). A base, foundational fabric of any society is the need to relate properly and in safe ways. A society that can't get along will ultimately unravel and fail, thus "bearing one another in love" is the opposite of anarchy. The modern reader, however, might be put off with such an old sounding term as "forbearing" or "bearing one another." Snodgrass modernizes the phrase using this structure: "putting up with one another in love" (197). Either way, the result should be a people set apart and led to treat others with a unique love (agape) and respect that stands out in any and all societies. Snodgrass adds,

> The focus on "one another" is significant. This word occurs forty times in Paul's letters. Christians are part of each other and are to receive one another, think about one another, serve one another, love one another, build up one another, bear each other's burdens, submit to each other, and encourage each other. Christianity is a God-directed, Christ-defined, other-oriented religion. Only with such direction away from self do we find ourselves. (197)

Unity and Peace (4:3)

In verse 3 Paul asks for, but doesn't command, unity based on the commonality of God's Spirit through the bond of peace. Why does he request and not command this unity and peace? "Paul often uses the word translated 'making every effort' for the effort and work in making a journey" (Arnold, 231). Arnold goes on to explain that Paul is really imploring the believers to maintain the original unity they were given when they accepted Jesus as Lord. The gift of the Holy Spirit provides unity with God that can and should naturally merge into relationships with other people. In this particular case, the unity requested is primarily within the church. In essence, if a church of Christians cannot find common-ground unity and peace within their own fellowship, how can they ever hope to make a positive impression among nonbelievers? Add in the fact that they have built-in assistance through the Holy Spirit, and the option of being divisive and fractious is indeed sad.

Perhaps the best way to read this request for unity based in peace is to see it as necessary in achieving the attributes found in the first two verses of chapter 4. Without an already present sense of unity, peace, and intertwined purpose, it would be difficult for so many people to live in genuine agape-love. Bonnie Thurston sees this as a form of "self-restraint" for the common good: "The 'unity of the Spirit in the bond of peace' (v. 3) provides the motive for such self-discipline. The Ephesians are called upon to be eager, to take pains or make every effort, to maintain their unity of Spirit in the peace that binds them together" (124).

Peace in the larger body originating from within each individual in the congregation was not a new concept, nor was it ever as being more corporate than personal. F. F. Bruce cites one of Paul's other letters in explaining the importance of unity and peace within the church:

> One body and one spirit echo 1 Cor. 12:13, which affirms the association between these two: in the one spirit the people of Christ have been baptized into the one body, the spirit being the animating principle of the corporate body of Christ. The unity of the Spirit is maintained as the members of the body function together harmoniously for the well-being of the whole. It was never envisaged as applicable to one local church only: wherever the people of Christ were found, there was his body, of which there were individually members. (336)

Simply put, being at peace with God must preface being at peace with other people.

One Body, One Spirit (4:4)

Have you ever wondered how many different Christian church varieties there are in existence today? Have you ever wondered if God meant for the church to have fragmented into so many iterations? Reading Paul's letters would lead us to surmise that God created "one" church and that one church was to be the vehicle to reconcile the world to God. There was to be one church powered by the one Spirit doing the work of the one God. The first three chapters of this epistle dealt with the theological underpinnings of God's overall unity provisions. Paul also wrote in Galatians that there would no longer be "male or female, Jew or Greek (Gentile)," as Jesus came to be the Savior of all people. The idea of complete oneness and unity is a must for understanding God's calling for the church.

> First, there is *one body* because there is *one Spirit*. The one body is the church, the body of Christ, comprising Jewish and Gentile believers; and its unity or cohesion is due to the one Holy Spirit who indwells and animates it. As Paul writes elsewhere, "By one Spirit we were all baptized into one body—Jews or Greeks, slaves or free—and all were made to drink of one Spirit. Thus, it is our common possession of the one Holy Spirit that integrates us into one body. (Stott, 150)

Peter O'Brien states that the church is the "local manifestation of this heavenly entity" (281), thus the church of Jesus Christ must be unified, whole, and at peace if it truly reflects the heavenly reality. How is this accomplished? Through God's Spirit is the only possible way for any individual or congregation to manifest peace and unity. Drop by a meeting of an average church committee and you will see the level of difficulty involved in a congregation being "one" and operating in a spirit of "peace." Barclay adds, "The word for spirit and breath in Greek is *pneuma*. Unless there is breath in the body; and the life-giving breath of the body of the church is the Spirit of Christ, there can be no church without the Spirit" (163).

One Lord, Faith, and Baptism (4:5)

It has been suggested that Paul is simply restating an older religious creed in these verses. While anything is possible, this is highly unlikely. Paul is making landmark statements; drawing the proverbial line in the sand; making a proclamation that Jesus is the Lord of all peoples, that there is but one faith and that baptism is the signature event that will set apart the people of God.

While there was but one church (catholic) in the early era, it's no secret that splits and schisms occurred as time went by. Have such fractures in the body of believers rendered this verse moot? The short answer would be no, that this verse remains in effect and pivotal to our theology and practice. Despite the reality that there are more Baptist offshoots than the number of people the average church in America has in attendance on any Sunday morning, we continue to have "one" faith based in and on Jesus Christ.

This is not to say that the thousands of fractures in the Protestant Christian wing of the faith was necessarily God's plan for his church. After reading the first three chapters of this epistle, one could be fairly certain that today's free-for-all mish-mash of church types was not what God had in mind when he left us in charge of the store. That said, we still exist under the banner of Jesus Christ as Lord and Savior, and we always will. Our reality may shift, change, and even split, but the heavenly reality is unalterable.

The act of baptism was hugely important to the early church. Baptism in early churches was primarily adults-only, as the majority of those who found faith in Jesus under Paul's ministry came from distinctly pagan backgrounds. Theirs was a profound statement of faith in Jesus and a renouncing of their former lives. Barclay makes an excellent comparison using Roman soldiers: "There was only one way for a Roman soldier to join the army: he had to take the oath that he would be forever true to his emperor. Similarly, there was only one way to enter the Christian Church—the way of public confession of Jesus Christ" (163). A. T. Robertson adds to the importance of this public display by stating that baptism is to "put Christ on in a public way" (535). Peter O'Brien ties it all together: "There is only one baptism because there is one Lord Jesus Christ in whom believers are united" (284).

One God and One Father (4:6)

Paul ends this section filled with acclamations with a focus on God as Father and echoing the words of 1 Corinthians 8:6: "yet for us there is but one God, the Father, from whom all things came and for whom we live." Both this Corinthians verse and Ephesians 4: 6 are reworkings of the Shema and place great importance on God being "over all, through all and in all." In writings such as these, it is easy to see God as being so high and lifted up, so lofty and "in" everything, that the possibility of God becoming a nebulous notion is real. Both Paul and the Shema (which Paul would have been greatly familiar with) were intended to place God above all pagan and assorted false gods being touted left and right. Today's believers take for granted that God is the One True God and the Creator of all. That reality would not have been in place in Ephesus or other locations where Paul strove to build churches on Gentile converts from cult/pagan religions.

Paul's repetitive proclamations that God is "over all, through all, and in all" was intended to show that God is indeed the God of the universe. There are commentators and theologians who reduce these words to the level of meaning only Christians, possibly Jews and

Gentiles, but a truly "cosmic" understanding of "all" seems more what Paul had in mind here. This makes even more sense when you look back to 3:14-15 where God is portrayed as Creator of all things and as such all things are dependent on him. This meshes into the overall theme of unity as one understands that God keeps the entire universe in place. Have you ever wondered how many moving parts there are in the universe? Or how many individual pieces there are to this massive puzzle we experience as life? God keeps it all moving forward somehow, in a form of unity that boggles our finite minds. We won't figure any of this out. We can't. We aren't capable of thinking at those levels. It's best to see God as being the God of all and ourselves as dependent on him for our existence. To do otherwise is simply foolishness.

This also allows us to see the church for what it was originally intended to be and, consequently, to place our roles in the proper perspective. The following words are helpful for anyone who has mistakenly lifted the church above the prescribed level:

> He is the Creator of all living things, so that their existence and significance depend on him. On this interpretation Paul is affirming that God is supremely transcendent "over everything" and that his immanence is all-pervasive: he works "through all in all." If this latter understanding is correct, then God's universal sovereignty and presence are set forth as the climactic ground for the unity of the Spirit that believers are to maintain. His universal rule is being exercised to fulfill his ultimate purpose of unifying all things in Christ. The unity of the church is the means by which the manifold wisdom of God is being displayed to the universe. The church is the eschatological outpost, the pilot project of God's purposes, and his people are the expression of this unity that displays to the universe his final goal. (O'Brien, 285–86)

Life Lessons

Paul shifts from teaching theology to giving practical instruction on the Christian lifestyle to his readers. Unity is a prime and foundational tenet of his instruction. Disunity and chaos defined the era Paul served, so pledging allegiance to the One God in a pagan, polytheistic world was indeed a bold statement. To actually and actively live out said allegiance was an even bigger task. Paul's focus on one faith, one church, one mission, and the equality of all people was difficult to live out in the mid-first century with Rome and fundamentalist

Jews looking over the shoulder of the new movement. Today? If we are honest, we must admit that in the modern West it is much easier to live out one's faith than in the time of Paul. Is there persecution in the West? To a small degree, but let's face it: we have it made in comparison to many other eras of history. Possibly our takeaway should be to embrace our freedom and seek to make the most of the opportunity by living out each virtue Paul mentions with a goal of influencing our society with the *positive* message of Christ. There is ample negativity in our society, and much of it comes from our churches. For the good news to be received as actually *good* news, it must be paired with positives. Imagine a society where patience, kindness, humility, and peace are lived out and shared. Paul did, and he believed it could become reality. It remains a worthy goal.

1. In light of today's multi-style, multi-church world, how would you explain Paul's teachings on unity within the body of Christ?

_____

_____

_____

_____

_____

2. Does Paul ever exalt the church over and above the individual believer? Explain your answer.

_____

_____

_____

_____

_____

3. Describe the differences between humility, meekness, and weakness.

_____

_____

_____

_____

_____

4. Do you agree that living at the midpoint of a virtue is the best way to live? Explain your response.

_____

_____

_____

_____

_____

5. List ways that modern Christians could model Christ by being more patient.

_____

_____

_____

_____

_____

6. In what ways could we do better in bearing one another in love? How would these actions promote agape-style love?

_____

_____

_____

_____

_____

7. Have you personally experienced a church suffering from disunity and discord? If so, list or discuss ways a discordant church becomes ineffective.

_____

_____

_____

_____

_____

8. List factors that often lead to discordant churches.

_____

_____

_____

_____

_____

9. Is baptism necessary for salvation? Has the need for baptism changed from the time of the early church?

_____

_____

_____

_____

_____

10. The early church faced a multi-cultural, multi-religion world. Today's church faces a multi-cultural, multi-religion world that is getting smaller each year. What can today's church learn from the early church about how to bring the message of Christ to today's world?

_____

_____

_____

_____

_____

6

Up, Down, and Getting Busy

Ephesians 4:7-16

Ascending and Descending

Verses 8-10 are three of the most debated, even fractious verses in Scripture. To be honest, no one really knows what Paul meant in these verses, so any dogmatic stances would be counterproductive to seeing all the possible meanings. The key to any applicable understanding is linked to verse 7 always being included in the reading. Allowing verse 7 to stand alone and apart from the unique following verses is moving even further away from Paul's original intentions. It's undeniable that Paul is teaching that gifts to believers are both a product and a result of Christ's descending and ascending and that he is using Psalm 68 as a bridge between the Testaments. The thorny questions arise when the exact meanings of "descend" and "lower earthly regions" are up for debate. Was Paul talking about a descent by Christ into Hell or Hades? Did he mean that Jesus came to earth to provide salvation to God's people? Could it possibly be what happened at Pentecost when the Spirit of God empowered the beginnings of the new church? Or was it entirely figurative in nature and merely a way to intertwine the two Testaments?

Clinton E. Arnold writes extensively on the first-century religious context of this section, stating that the average reader or hearer of these words would interpret it as a literal trip into Hades. He writes that "underworld themes were prominent in Ephesus where a prominent goddess was Hekate, goddess of witchcraft and sorcery, who held the keys to Hades. Often depicted holding keys, Hekate was believed to have the power to lock and unlock the gates of Hades, thus controlling the demons held there" (254). This view is supported by Revelation 1:18, where Jesus is praised as the one who "bears the keys of death and Hades." If Paul did indeed have this meaning in mind, it could have been successful in reaching the people of Ephesus who were hyper-aware of the evil of demonic goddesses and other malevolent cult figures. This view has been invalidated by modern theologians who (rightly) point out that Paul neglects to mention Hades and uses the much less specific "lower regions of the earth."

If Paul simply meant that Jesus descended to the "lower parts of the earth" by coming to earth then this is not a dilemma at all. O'Brien is a proponent of this view and suggests that the best interpretation is "descended to the earth below" (294). Stott rounds out this view by removing any spatial elements and referring only to the amazing amount of debasement Jesus must have felt by allowing himself to come to earth in the form of a person: "What is in Paul's mind is not so much descent and ascent in spatial terms, but rather humiliation and exaltation, the latter bringing Christ universal authority and power" (159).

Captivating the Captives (4:8)

Suffice it to say we do not know exactly what Paul meant in his teachings on Christ's descending, but we do know what the end results have been. Tying in Psalms 68, we can see how the victorious King has defeated his enemies and bestowed gifts upon his people. This is what Jesus did with the dissemination of the various spiritual gifts (and certainly the ultimate gifts of salvation and the indwelling Holy Spirit). Another parallel is in place with the words of verse 8: "When he ascended on high, he led captives in his train and gave gifts to men" (also Ps 68:18). According to the Life Application Bible Commentary, these words have one of two possible meanings: (1) he led the captured ones (as one would lead a train of vanquished foes) into their captivity, or (2) he captured the captors (that is, he reversed the captivity; he enslaved the enslavers). Both meanings imply that Christ vanquished our enemies (such as death, Satan, and sin) and captivated them (80).

Taking the entire section as a whole, it is easy to see that the second option is the best fit. Jesus descended to the area where evil exists and not only defeated it; he enslaved it. Timothy G. Gombis sums it up with a quintessentially biblical twist: "The best explanation for the identity of these hostile warriors that Christ defeated is the principalities, powers and authorities" (375). Written in this manner, it comes across as both an amazingly powerful statement on God's plans through Jesus and as an age-old morality play that would have appealed to the first-century Greco-Romans. The imagery of a powerful and victorious king returning from battle and bestowing gifts on his people stands the test of time. We as humans resonate on "good" defeating "evil," especially when it is played out on such a cosmic level.

Spiritual Gifts (4:11-12)

Paul shifts from a focus on corporate church unity to one of individuality within the body of Christ. There may be "one" church, but it is made up of individuals who have proclaimed faith in Jesus Christ and subsequently been gifted by God's Spirit for service. In essence, Paul is making a sharp turn toward the inner workings of the "one" church.

> Although the church is one unified body, each of its members has a special gift to be used for the good and growth of all. No one is overlooked; everyone is important to building up the community. God in his wisdom did not make believers photocopies of one another. Instead, each believer has at least one special ability, given according to the generosity of Christ, to be used to accomplish the work of the Kingdom. (Barton et al., 819)

Steve Motyer writes that the gifts do not undermine the unity of the church; rather, diversity of gifts builds a unified ministry (114). His observation is key in understanding the true theology of the church. Most people would agree that today's church does not resemble the early church in the least. That elementary reality, however, also demonstrates much of what is wrong with the modern versions of the church. It's extremely trite to state that many to most of today's churches are basically spectator events that meet once per week for an hour or so. The work of the church is done by a staff of highly educated clergy and trained volunteers who make up a small percentage of the church's membership. The early churches met in homes many times each week, were relatively small in number, and saw their mission as reaching people for Jesus. Paul wrote about spiritual gifts in each of his letters to churches to assist in making sure each believer found his or her active role in promoting the faith.

Paul writes that the victorious Jesus bestowed five specific gifts on his church: "It was he who gave some to be apostles, some to be prophets, some to be evangelists, and some to be pastors and teachers" (4:11). William Barclay emphasizes the importance of this short section as it provides a picture of the administration and organization of the early church (167). It's important to note that the full gamut of spiritual gifts must be pulled together from various other New Testament epistles, and the complete list would reach twenty unique gifts. Paul only lists four specific gifts in this epistle, but it's obvious that these gifts were prominent and would have been important for both authority and structure within the new movement.

APOSTLES

Generally an apostle was a person who "saw" Jesus either before or after the resurrection. In the strictest definition, this would include a very small number of people. In a more general sense, an apostle could also be seen as an envoy, a representative or a person sent on a specific mission. This less restrictive definition would obviously increase the number of possible people who held this early position. It would stand to reason that as the early disciples/apostles died, the less restrictive view would have been needed. One would have to at least consider both Timothy and Titus as apostles who were sent by Paul to Ephesus and Crete respectively. As Arnold states, "Christ is continuing to give these leaders to the church for the equipping of the individual members and facilitating their growth and maturity" (256). This is thus a progressive appointment process that would move the role of apostle from those who had seen Jesus to those expressly set apart and called by God to serve. A simple way to describe this first-century position would be to see it as a person sent on a mission. This office would transcend the local church and be a traveling emissary for the faith. Barnabas is an excellent example of an apostle of this era.

PROPHETS

New Testament prophets did not have the same roles as Old Testament prophets. In the Hebrew texts, prophets wrote and proclaimed messages pertaining to the future, specifically those tied to judgment due for Israel's prolonged sin. The New Testament prophets were those who spoke "for the strengthening, encouragement and comfort" of people (1 Cor 14:3). It's possible to see these people as church planters who went in early and proclaimed the positives made available by Christ. It's important to note that at the time of Paul's writing, the New Testament was not in the form we know it today. There were letters such as this epistle that often found their way from church to church. In many cases, it was the prophet who would provide interpretation and application of these letters for the believers in one church and then another church. This position was an itinerant one in the early church.

A common question today is "where have the prophets gone?" Today's church does not seem to offer the position of prophet among its ranks of professional clergy. Seminaries today do not offer an academic track for the role of prophet. R. Kent Hughes believes this role ceased being necessary when the New Testament came together, after which pastors and teachers were given the primary roles of interpretation, exhortation, proclamation, and application: "The apostles and prophets were given to the church to get her established, but now their role is assumed by the canonical writings of the New Testament. The apostles and prophets with their unique endowments did not extend beyond the apostolic age" (133).

EVANGELISTS

This role in the early church was given to those with the gift of taking the news of the resurrection and gospel story to new people and places, particularly to the uninitiated. While Paul could easily be seen as being multi-gifted, he would certainly fulfill the gifted role of an evangelist. This particular noun appears only three times in the New Testament (here, Acts 21:8, and 2 Timothy 4:5) and in each case has to do with the spreading of the gospel. Barclay identifies this group as being less prestigious than either apostles or prophets, but they were nonetheless important missionaries "who took the good news to a world which had never heard it" (169). O'Brien sees evangelists serving multi-purpose roles "preaching the gospel, planting churches and working with established congregations." He adds, "evangelists were to have a ministry to believers and unbelievers alike" (299).

PASTORS AND TEACHERS

Strangely, "pastor" is used only in Ephesians to refer distinctly to an office in the church. Other versions and variations occur, specifically "shepherds," "overseers," and "elders," but it is clear Paul that had a local intent in mind with this verse. The Life Application Commentary agrees by stating that early pastors functioned much like "shepherds who tended God's flock in the local church" (83). It is possible that the pastor would provide care and structure and the teacher would do the obvious: teach. This would mean that what we know of today as preaching was not a regular facet of the very early church. The style would have been modeled on either the rabbinic method of seated teaching or the grander oratory inspired by the Greeks (Apollos would be an example of this style). A natural question arises at this point: was this one position/person serving in both roles, or were there two different leaders called to different ministries?

Bickel and Jantz speak for a large number of commentators who believe it was common to have a "teaching pastor" who served in the duals of teacher and shepherd in a local church (102). Neither John Stott nor John Calvin agree, instead seeing these roles as being separate gifts held by different individuals: "the administration of discipline, the sacraments, warnings and exhortation belonged particularly to pastors, and feeding of the flock is done by teachers" (Stott, 163). Perhaps Bonnie Thurston says it best (and most succinctly): "Pastors and teachers, whose functions are related, work with those already in the household of faith. Teachers are to give instruction in the faith, and pastors to give care" (125).

Oh Grow Up! (4:13-16)

The next section exhorts the Ephesians to see their unity leading to a maturing faith that will stand the tests of life and increasing persecution. To say life was difficult for these early Christians would be grand understatement. They faced hostility from Rome, the Jewish establishment, the various pagan religions, and often their own families. For the movement to make it into the second century would require these believers to grow up and mature in their faith quickly and correctly. Paul was asking for their newly understood unity to lead to an intensely focused hunger for a new life based on Jesus.

A key to understanding these verses is the manner in which the verb "attain" is used. In this case it literally means "to come to meet," and implies that unity is both a gift given by Christ and a goal they/we must strive for. Possibly the best tack is to see this section citing that the possibility for unity is a supernatural gift provided by the victorious Christ. Experiencing unity is not a foregone conclusion. It is a state the entire church must work through the Holy Spirit to achieve and, much like salvation, it's a process in constant flux. Again the key is to strive to make the flux stable and positive in direction. Salvation is best described as "I am saved; I am being saved; I will be saved." The same can be said for progressive unity: "I am seeking unity; we are seeking unity; we will all be unified."

A consistent theme in Paul's letters is the need for spiritual stability and the ability to stay strong in the midst of false teaching. There were many competing philosophies floating around the Greco-Roman world in the mid-late first century. Many of the philosophies found their way into the church, and the results were often disastrous. Gnosticism is an example of a false, pseudo-religious teaching that wreaked havoc in many Gentile Christian congregations. By seeking spiritual maturity, these early believers would be in a better position to withstand the competing, often more attractive options. Snodgrass sees Paul's use of "tossed back and forth" and "blown here and there" as representing "being easily deceived, tricked and not being able to determine genuine truth" (206). He also does an excellent job in defining the unique use of love in verse 15: "One summarizes what Christian living is all about: truth, love and continual growth into Christ in everything. The word for 'truth' here is actually a verb; a literal translation is 'truthing in love.' The thought that *the truth is something one does* occurs in the Old Testament, in the New Testament, and in the Qumran scrolls" (206).

Essentially this section means that Christ is the head of the church, the church is the body, and each person/part serves a purpose. What is the end goal of the body? A verb-like faith that exhibits itself in the distinct form of love. Love is to be a verb, not merely a feeling or an emotion. What is our best example of love as a verb? Jesus on the cross and in the resurrection. Love in action. Love in verb form. This is the goal of our unity and our spiritual growth.

Life Lessons

Paul tackled one of the most debated issues of the New Testament in citing Jesus' descent into "the lower regions." Since no one today fully understands these verses, it's safe to admit that fact and settle for what we do know: that Jesus defeated death and dealt evil a permanent setback. The larger beauty is that Jesus did all he did for *us*. In defeating death and providing for our sin penalty, he gave the church a track to run on in continuing to fulfill God's mission. Of course, it is true that the church has been its own worst enemy more times than not, and we tend to run off-track for selfish reasons. To be successful, the church must exist as one body living out a unified message. It must be led and facilitated by apostles who live missional lives, by prophets, or, in our vernacular, by church planters who progress the church one new fellowship at a time, evangelists who proclaim the gospel, and pastor-teachers who provide care and instruction to the members. The New Testament church is the vehicle God has used for reaching and redeeming the world.

Paul also stressed the pivotal need for unity among the believers. The mission would only be successful if the church remained together, strong and on task. Not one word Paul penned to the Ephesian church is dated or without modern application. The church remains more powerful than evil. The church continues to need called and set-apart leaders. And, most important, the church must be unified to its core if it is to be successful. To fail in any of Paul's requirements for the church is to fail God and limit the kingdom's work.

1. Is unity as important in today's church as it was in the early church? How might spiritual maturity lead to more unity?

_____

_____

_____

_____

_____

2. In what ways are the early church and today's church similar? Dissimilar?

_____

_____

_____

_____

_____

3. Are you familiar with the teaching that Jesus descended into Hades/Hell to preach to the inhabitants? What would be the purpose of such a visit?

_____

_____

_____

_____

_____

4. How was Jesus humiliated by coming to earth and dwelling with humanity?

_____

_____

_____

_____

_____

5. Why do you think Paul listed only five of the possible twenty spiritual gifts?

_____
_____
_____
_____
_____

6. What is the difference between a talent and a spiritual gift?

_____
_____
_____
_____
_____

7. What does it mean to our faith and theology that Jesus captured the powers and principalities of sin and death?

_____
_____
_____
_____
_____

8. What is a modern example of false teaching that is problematic for immature Christians and subsequently the church?

_____
_____
_____
_____
_____

Don't Be So Gentile

Ephesians 4:17-32

Paul has made the case for unity in the church and in personal theology, and now he begins a wholesale shift to the ethical mandates for personal living. In classic Paul-phraseology, Gentiles are instructed not to live like Gentiles. While this may sound strange to us, these early non-Jewish Christians understood exactly what Paul was teaching. He consistently taught that a conversion to faith in Jesus Christ requires a symbolic death to the former "natural" self. Paul taught that a duality exists between the natural and the redeemed person who has become new through Christ. Once a choice is made to follow Christ, a person is to see the "old" and "former" self as symbolically dead. The "new" person experiences a new life provided by Jesus and powered by the Holy Spirit. Second Corinthians 5:17 speaks to this new life: "What this means is that those who become Christians become new persons. They are not the same anymore, for the old life is gone. A new life has begun!" Jantz and Bickel add, "As a new Christian, you have a new spiritual nature" (109).

Sadly, our former selves are not taken into cosmic custody. We are very much stuck with the frailties and foibles of our nature and our tendency toward sin. Our sin state is in constant conflict with our new spiritual nature. Paul admonishes the newly converted Greeks and Romans that the world they formally inhabited must become alien in as many ways as possible. The old ways of thinking are futile, he says, so stay away from the heady arguments and philosophies that seek to explain the meaning of life. Hedonism is to be a practice of the past life and must not be grafted into their new faith in Christ. It's helpful to note that Ephesus was home to a magnificent temple dedicated to Diana, the goddess of love. Much like Corinth, where temple prostitutes were on duty 24/7, the combination of sex and religion was seen as paying homage to the gods and goddesses. In short, Paul calls the Ephesian believers to note the stark contrasts between their former pagan lives and their new lives in Christ. He is profoundly negative in his critique of common Gentile beliefs and practices, but his reasoning is good: to call for a line of separation between the old and new life that will be a measuring stick for the rest of their lives.

> The vividness of Paul's descriptive terminology serves both to explicate his ideas and to elicit a response from the readers/ hearers. There is an emotive content to words like *futility* (v. 17); *darkened, separated, ignorance, hardening* (v. 18); *sensitivity, sensuality, indulge, lust* (v. 19). When this is combined with the intellectual content of the words *thinking* and *understanding* the total picture is clear. It also forms a contrast to "speaking the truth in love" (v. 15). (Liefeld, 112)

The Walk (4:17)

An old adage states that people see sermons more than they hear sermons. The idea is obviously that the way Christians live their outward lives has a more profound impact on unbelievers than sermons, songs, or books ever will. Paul is asking the Gentile Christians to live lives that will be in stark contrast to those of their fellow Gentiles.

"Paul wants their attitudes and conduct to become sharply differentiated from the non-Christian Greeks and Romans with whom they live" (Arnold, 281). The Greek word used by Paul for "walk" is very Hebrew in nature and implies an all-encompassing lifestyle based on a reverent fear of God. The writer of Ecclesiastes describes the Hebrew view of the human quest for knowledge and wisdom:

> I, the teacher, was king over Israel in Jerusalem. I applied my mind to study and to explore by wisdom all that is done under the heavens. What a heavy burden God has laid on mankind! I have seen all the things that are done under the sun; all of them are meaningless, a chasing after the wind. What is crooked cannot be straightened out; what is lacking cannot be counted. I said to myself, "Look, I have increased in wisdom more than anyone who has ruled over Jerusalem before me; I have experienced much of wisdom and knowledge." Then I applied myself to the

understanding of wisdom, and also of madness and folly, but I learned that this, too, is a chasing after the wind. For with much wisdom comes more sorrow; the more knowledge, the more grief. (1:12-18)

It's important to note that Paul was not saying that the highly intelligent and forward-thinking Greeks and Romans were futile in all of their thinking. History demonstrates that the Greeks and Romans provided the world with unprecedented gains in many fields. What he was stating was spiritually based. No one then and no one today can successfully harness God's creations. Today's brightest minds admit to knowing only a portion of how the human brain works. The universe continues to be larger than our capacity to grasp its complexities. We may be smart, but we aren't smart enough to *find* God intellectually.

Blind Hearts (4:18)

Being true to his Hebrew roots, Paul speaks to a "darkened mind." Hebrews regularly referred to themselves as sighted and Gentiles as being blind. In effect this is a continuation of that metaphor, as they have become blind to the futility of both their thinking and their endeavors. The darkened minds have also led to hardened hearts. The Greek work for "hardness" is literally "petrified" in English. In the first century, the definition described that level of hardness as a "stone harder than marble" (Stott, 176). Another view was a medical one referring to a callus. "The moral point is that, having done wrong repeatedly, the Gentiles no longer think of their actions as wrong. The conscience has become calloused, petrified" (Thurston, 128–29). Snodgrass explained it this way:

> The Gentiles are separated from God because of deliberate ignorance, which has taken residence in their souls. The Gentiles are ignorant because of their hardness of heart. The heart is the source of all loyalties. In this case hardness of heart has prevented all loyalty to God. In sum, hearts made insensitive to God have set off a chain reaction that turned out the lights and led to meaningless. (230–31)

Paul also cites the "ignorance that is within them" to demonstrate the differences between Gentile Christians and unbelievers who continue in humanistic and pagan practices and beliefs. This isn't scornful in the sense of today's usage of "ignorant." Ignorant here essentially means a specific lack of knowledge. The pagan Gentiles Paul contrasts are simply lacking an understanding of what a personal relationship with God through Jesus means. There is a void in their capacity to comprehend God's amazing grace, peace, and purpose. The Gentile Christians have this knowledge and are being told to not squander it and slip back to the level of ignorant, unbelieving Gentiles. Obviously this is occurring, or Paul wouldn't go to the lengths he does to correct their behavior. Much the same happens in the Corinth church, and Paul is even firmer in that letter. Ignorance, hardened hearts, and spiritual blindness are a sure path to gross sin.

Lust, Sensuality, and Lack of Feeling (4:19)

The penalty of a darkened and petrified mind and soul is an insatiable desire for more and more impure things. Today's church would understand this two-thousand-year-old verse as well as the original hearers did. If one sins and has no capacity to see it as wrong, he or she will continue to sin. The downside, although the pagan Gentiles would not have likely seen any downside to their condition, is the factor of insatiability. In a Greco-Roman culture of sanctioned depravity, the Gentile Christians had to be on guard against slipping back to their former lives of "self-first sensuality." The pagans in Ephesus have an excuse of sorts in that a licentious lifestyle is all they have ever known. Not so for the freshly minted Christians, who know the differences and have crossed to the other side. If they go backwards, they will damage themselves and God's kingdom.

The Jews see idolatry as the root of all sin and rebellion against God. Paul doesn't stray from that foundational belief; he says that continual lust is insatiable. Knowing that only God can truly satisfy, catering to out-of-control self-satisfaction is an exercise in making an idol of oneself. As Snodgrass writes, "These verses reflect a Jewish understanding of idolatry as the root of all sin, and greed as the sin encompassing all sins. Impure activity is rooted in greedy desire" (231).

Christ the Teacher (4:20-21)

Paul makes a quick shift to restate the fact that each and every Gentile Christian in Ephesus has had opportunity to learn about Christ and his life. If Paul were still writing to churches today, he might say, "It's not like this is *rocket science*, people!" Arnold sums up this argument with these words: "In sharp contrast to the prevailing way of non-Christian thinking and living, Paul reminds his readers that they have learned a different way. Through their personal relationship with Jesus Christ, they have a new identity and an entirely new way to live that is shaped by Christ and his teaching" (284). Liefeld makes one of the strongest observations to date in stating that "the central truth of Christianity does not reside mainly in its creeds or sacraments but in Jesus himself" (114).

Tossing Off the Old Clothes (4:22)

Paul consistently uses the metaphor of old versus new to describe the before-and-after versions of Christians. Read any of Paul's epistles and you'll find him stating that the old life is to be put away and never again to be entertained:

> Do not lie to each other, since you have taken off your old self with its practices and have put on the new self, which is being renewed in knowledge in the image of its Creator. (Col 3:9-10)

> Or don't you know that all of us who were baptized into Christ Jesus were baptized into his death? . . . For we know that our old self was crucified with him so that the body of sin might be done away with, that we should no longer be slaves to sin. (Rom 6:3, 6)

> You are all sons of God through faith in Christ Jesus, for all of you who were baptized into Christ have clothed yourselves with Christ. (Gal 3:26-27)

These verses form a type of baptismal theology. The act of baptism is a symbolic dying to the "old, former" person, and rising to a new life. The water is used to symbolize the cleansing from one's sin condition. Obviously this act won't keep future sin at bay, nor will it, in and of itself, provide salvation. It becomes a line of demarcation, a point in time for a person to revisit mentally for the assurances of salvation and the ability to withstand the temptations of returning to the former life. It's important to note that to be successful in following Christ, one must live a lifestyle of constantly putting off the old life.

> . . . in verse 22 Paul in effect challenges them to a repeated putting off of the old garments, the old style of life. Scripture and

experience teach us that no one has ever succeeded in shedding the garments of the old life with a solitary, unrepeated action. Those who live holy lives do so by repeated putting offs. The problem is that the old garments are so comfortable and natural. Not only that, many of us have worn them so long that they naturally drape over us and we scarcely know we are wearing them until the Holy Spirit reproves us. (Hughes, 143)

Toward a New Mind (4:23)

When Paul writes, "and be renewed in the spirit of your mind," is he referring to a renewal powered by God's Spirit, or is the responsibility on the individual believer? The easy route would be to place all responsibility on the Holy Spirit, but the construction of the verse doesn't allow for this option. As is the norm with Paul, the Ephesian Christians are given the responsibility of taking charge of their own minds. In the letters to Timothy, "spirit" is synonymous with "attitude," but here it seems to mean the human spirit or, put another way, the human's ongoing mental practices. Paul is instructing the Ephesians that what they think and how they use their minds will determine their decisions. Taken a step further, their long-term success as followers of Christ will be determined in great part by how they uses their minds. Snodgrass sees the human mind as "the object of continued renewal" (235).

The Holy Man (4:24)

Paul uses a second word for new in this verse as he raises the bar on the call for consistent holy living. James also uses a form of "new" that requires explanation as simple languages like English have no equivalent. Think of something we would consider as being new, like an automobile or television. While the new automobile may be new to *us*, it is not new in concept. Anyone alive today has seen an automobile, and they've likely seen one on television. Neither would be a new reality. Paul is stressing a new that is heretofore unknown, an entirely new reality brought about by an entirely new process. Before Jesus, no one had been a living example of sinless perfection or of infinite *agape*-love. With the ascension of Jesus and the coming of the Holy Spirit, this new newness was made available to all people.

The two truths of this verse and the last need to be kept before the Christian. As Westcott puts it, "Two things are required for the positive formation of the Christian character, the continuous and progressive renewal of our highest faculty, and the decisive acceptance of the "new man."" This *new nature* is *created after the likeness of God.* (Foulkes, 139)

Steve Motyer adds an interesting touch to this verse packed with both theological and practical importance:

> Paul is thinking back to 2:15, where he spoke of the "one new person" which Christ has created in himself, bringing together Jews and Gentiles into a whole new body, the church. A new creation, a new "person," a new type of being. To "put" on this new creation, a new "person" means *actually to become, in practice, what God intends this new human being to be like.* He intends us to be like himself—marked by *righteousness* and *holiness.* (130)

So "to be like Christ" has to be more than a lofty stanza in a hymn or an impressive line in a creed; it must become a daily rallying cry for the Christian and the first step in the daily exercise of "putting off the old person" and "putting on the new creation clothed in righteousness and holiness." This simple verse could/should become item 1 on our daily to-do list.

Speaking Truth (4:25)

The explicit command here is to "stop lying," although Paul uses the lighter "speaking truth with your neighbor." While John Stott suggests that this verse might point to the larger issue of standing for the one true faith in Jesus over the various pagan religions (based on Paul's "great lie of idolatry" in Rom 1:25; p. 185), most commentators pursue the basic angle of personal trustworthiness in all things, primarily interpersonal speech. Relationships cannot withstand consistent untruthfulness. If lies infiltrate the church, Christian community will be negatively affected. A Christian who lies in the marketplace will bring dishonor on God and the church. Any and all forms of lying are condemned. This is an all-inclusive injunction: cease all lies and replace the lies with truth.

> The command is not merely negative, but positive. It is not enough to cease lying; *falsehood* must be replaced by truth. This is especially appropriate given the introductory statement about

"the truth that is in Jesus" (v. 21). The *neighbor* in this case is presumably a Christian, given the casual clause that follows, *for we are all members of one body.* It forwards Paul's concern with the unity of the body. Falsehood divides; truth unites. (Liefeld, 116)

Paul is also inferring that a decision to speak the truth is one we face multiple times each day. To lie or not to lie is, and always will be, a choice to be made by any person in control of his or her faculties. The choice of a lie over the truth is in play daily, and when the choice is made to lie, it becomes progressively harder to undo the choice. Plus, just like any other negative in life, lying leads to additional lying and so on and so forth. Serial lying begins with the first lie. In the same vein, consistent and trustworthy truthfulness begins with the first truthful statement.

Anger with No Sin (4:26)

This short statement is one of the most difficult to defend in all of Scripture. James says much the same thing in 1:19-20: "My dear brothers, take note of this: Everyone should be quick to listen, slow to speak and slow to become angry, for man's anger does not bring about the righteous life God desires."

Both James and Paul, one the leader of the Jewish-Christian wing of the church and the other in the corresponding Gentile-Christian wing, say that one can become angry but must not allow the anger to become sin. To say that the line between anger and sin is thin is understatement, yet we are consistently told never to cross that line. Add to this that Jesus became visibly and demonstratively angry yet remained sinless and perfect, and the quandary deepens. How does a person experience anger but not allow sin to emerge as a result? Clinton Arnold believes Paul saw an appropriateness for anger but also a need for any/all anger to be dealt with quickly, lest it end in sin: "He (Paul) cautions that it is best to deal with it quickly, because if anger is left unchecked, it can make one susceptible to the attack of the evil one" (300). Put another way, if anger is allowed to fester, bad decisions and outcomes will likely result.

A rather large question arises at this point: what situations are worthy of anger, and how should Christians properly deal with anger? There is certainly no consensus on answers to these thorny questions. Jesus said "everyone who is angry with his brother shall be liable to judgment" (Matt 5:22). Jesus is portrayed as being angry with Israel in his encounter with the fig tree and with the outer-court temple merchants. He cursed the fig tree; he tossed around the merchandise and ran off the merchants. He became angry and he reacted, albeit quickly, and obviously his anger was kingdom oriented. But what about garden-variety, everyday anger? What about the often used line, "I'm not angry; I'm righteously indignant"? Perhaps F. F. Bruce has the best take on this uniquely different verse:

> How is it possible to "be angry without sinning" (Psalm 4:4)? There is no doubt a proper place for righteous indignation; but there is a subtle temptation to regard my anger as righteous indignation and other people's anger as sheer bad temper. Here it is suggested that anger can be prevented from degenerating into sin if a strict time limit is placed on it: "do not let the sun set on your anger." Let reconciliation be effected by nightfall, if possible. If that is not possible—if the person with whom one is angry is not accessible, or refuses to be reconciled—then at least the heart should be unburdened of its animosity by the committal of the matter to God. (361)

Of course, the better option is to work toward the goal of eradicating anger from one's life. If you stop and think about it, much of our anger centers on small, often inconsequential matters. When is the last time one of us became angry over child exploitation or disease-ridden areas where children have little to no expectancy for long-term survival? Sadly, most of us would remember anger over something small, temporary, and annoying. Our anger is miscast and misdirected in most cases, and we seem to entertain it as a way of life. This practice isn't spiritually beneficial or biblically based. In the end, anger's damage is entirely self-inflicted.

> Of the seven deadly sins, anger is possibly the most fun. To lick your wounds, to smack your lips over grievances long past, to roll over your tongue the prospect of bitter confrontation still to come, to savor to the last toothsome morsel both the pain you are given and the pain you are giving back; in many ways it is a feast fit for a king. The chief drawback is that what you are wolfing down is yourself. The skeleton at the feast is you. (Buechner, 2)

Devil: Keep Out (4:27)

It is not difficult to see anger as the quintessential slippery slope toward more and deeper sin. Paul certainly did as he tied prolonged, unrequited anger to an open door for the devil to take hold of the believer's life. There is some confusion over the translation of "devil" in this verse. Paul normally used "Satan" rather than "the devil," which has led some highly notable commentators (Erasmus and Luther) to see Paul meaning the more specific translation *diabolos*, or slanderer in Greek. Placed into its full context, it seems proper to view Paul's intent as "the devil" and that anger is a sin particularly constructed to allow evil to retake hold of our lives. Snodgrass states, "Anger is one place of inroad for him, a Trojan horse for his attack" (250).

Anger left unchecked and empowered by adversarial evil is not only a problem for interpersonal relationships. Bad blood can also strain and permanently stain a congregation. Look back far enough in any church that's fractured and split, and you'll likely find selfishness and anger. Again, left unchecked, anger will grow, and given enough time it will destroy the fellowship.

> The third exhortation in relation to anger, *do not give the devil a foothold* (v. 27), provides the motivation for dealing with anger promptly. If it is prolonged, Satan can use it for his own ends, exploiting the strains that develop within the Christian community. The word rendered *foothold*, literally means "place," but can signify "possibility, opportunity or chance" (Acts 25:16). Accordingly, the verse may be translated, "Do not give the devil a chance to exert his influence." (O'Brien, 340)

Suffice it to say, we are our own worst enemies when it comes to petty emotional issues. There's no reason we should allow the devil to make us worse. Knowing there's so much on the line, we should heed the words of Paul to the Ephesian Christians and work on our anger issues, realizing how close we are to entertaining evil each day.

Thou Shalt Not Steal (4:28)

Paul's third ethical command is very Hebrew in nature, almost straight from the eighth commandment (Exod 20:15). This is a familiar teaching from Paul, as he said essentially the same thing to the Romans (13:9) and Corinthians (1 Cor 6:10). Apparently stealing was quite common in Ephesus in that era as Paul was making more than a garden-variety admonition. It could easily be read that "the thief" should stop stealing and opt instead for hard work. Paul is instructing that any new Christian must give up their former, obviously sinful lifestyle. The thief must stop taking the easy route and actually earn his money and possessions. Christians will be known for good deeds not criminal activity, and they will be known as trustworthy, hardworking citizens.

> But when a thief becomes a Christian, he will not only give up stealing: he will do what he can to earn an honest livelihood and have something to give to those in need. The grace of generosity is part and parcel of the Christian way of life (Luke 6:29-36; 2 Corinthians 8:1-15; 9:6-12), but when practiced by a former thief it stands in total contrast to his previous life. To "work with one's own hands" is a favorite expression of Paul; in recommending such activity to others, he set an example himself. (Bruce, 362)

Filthy Talk (4:29)

Today we think of "filthy" talk as language filled with profanity. Paul is using *filthy* in a much different manner: "The basic meaning is 'rotten' or 'putrid.' It was used to refer to rotted wood, diseased lungs, rancid fish, withered flowers, and rotten fish" (Arnold, 304). While it could include profanity, which literally means "outside the temple," it is much more inclusive. Any admonition never to use language "outside the temple" that you wouldn't use inside the temple, sanctuary, cathedral, synagogue, or church is both prudent and positive. Additionally, Paul is teaching we must stay away from unwholesome, negative, demeaning, and derogatory speech—especially any of the aforementioned aimed at other people. In its place we are to adopt edifying speech that always aims to build up and support other people. John Stott explains,

> When applied to rotten talk, whether this is dishonest, unkind or vulgar, we may be sure that in some way it hurts the hearers. Instead, we are to use our unique gift of speech constructively, *for edifying*, that is to build people up and not damage or destroy them, *as fits the occasion.* Then our words will *impart grace to those who hear.* (188)

Grieving the Holy Spirit (4:30)

This verse strikes fear in people who wonder if they are capable of committing the unpardonable sin. But Paul did not have in mind anything close to the possibility of lashing out at God and blaspheming the Spirit. At its essence, he is saying that our full demeanor, especially our speech habits, can grieve God's Spirit who was given to us as our guide and spiritual conscience. Arnold writes, "rotten talk is not only harmful to the health of the Christian community; it grieves the Spirit of God" (306). O'Brien adds, "The Spirit is grieved when God's people continue in any of the sins that divide and destroy the unity of the body" (346).

Thomas Hale sees this verse as the culmination of the entire section: "it is really a joining together of all of our 'old behaviors' into one. The Spirit is grieved by every kind of unholiness" (743). We should be mindful that our sin damages God and drives a wedge between our lives and God's Spirit. Sin blocks all of the positives God provides for us through the Spirit. The possibility for peace and purpose is bleak if unconfessed sin stands between the individual believer and God. This is called a drift, and it's important to note that God never moves away from us; we do the shifting, and our direction is backwards.

Unwholesome to Wholesome (4:31-32)

Apparently the speech issues affecting the Ephesus church were profound. Paul wouldn't have pulled this specific teaching out of the air; some bad things were taking place within the church, or these negatives were beginning to infiltrate the church from the local culture. It is also of note that he isn't talking about general grumpiness or bad moods. "Clamor" is often defined as shouting and brawling, so it's easy to see why Paul wouldn't want this to occur in the church. "Slander" is a strong derogatory, and "malice" portends intent to do harm. These hyper-negatives are to be done away with in the lives of Christians and replaced by positive and uplifting interpersonal practices.

The opposite of a malicious, brawling, and slanderous person is a forgiving, loving, and tenderhearted soul. Paul takes the verse "and they will know us by our love" as a way of life, especially in pagan areas like Ephesus. To be wholesome in speech and demeanor would be to set oneself apart in a troubled, pagan-infested city like Ephesus.

Life Lessons

Paul's former Hebrew life as part of the Sanhedrin shines through in the Ephesian letter. It is obvious he is an intellectual and a scholar and understands the ways of God (to the degree anyone can know God's ways). His theological underpinnings in the first half of the letter create the framework for a life based in Christ that is so counter to the societal norm it would draw attention and interest. Of course, the Gentile Christians would have to live consistently for Christ among other Gentiles who, as Paul states, lived like "Gentiles." Paul is again shooting for a "before and after" line of demarcation so the Ephesians will always know how far they have come and have a basic life template to go by. He is brutal in his designations of the average unbelieving Ephesian who has a petrified heart, is addicted to lust and sensuality, is prone to lying and stealing, brawls and lives an angry life, is crude and profane in speech, and is untrustworthy.

Paul instructs his readers to live in the light rather than the dark, decaying, and destructive ways of the Gentiles. In essence he is teaching Gentiles not to be so Gentile because they have been redeemed in, and by, Christ. Our takeaway is basically the same: do not live like the average human; we have been made different through Christ. Non-Christian Gentiles in Ephesus were living from their base nature. The average person is doing exactly the same thing today. But as believers, our base nature has been redeemed, and we must live consistently from our "new" nature. This reality hasn't changed in the two millennia since Paul wrote this letter.

1. Describe how the public life of a Christian can be more powerful than a sermon.

_____

_____

_____

_____

_____

2. How is it possible for an educated, intellectual person to have darkened and futile thinking?

_____

_____

_____

_____

_____

3. List causes of backsliding. Discuss practical ways to keep from backsliding.

_____

_____

_____

_____

_____

4. Describe ways sinning can lead to insatiable desires that grow in magnitude and the long-term effect the desires can have on a person's life.

_____

_____

_____

_____

_____

5. Is it still possible to make an idol of oneself? Explain.

_____

_____

_____

_____

_____

6. Explain the baptismal example of the old versus new life as you would to a non-Christian.

_____

_____

_____

_____

_____

7. List practical ways people can renew their minds. Is it possible to live in a state of continual renewal? Explain your answer.

_____

_____

_____

_____

_____

8. How prevalent is lying in our culture? Is any form of lying acceptable for Christians? Is there really such a thing as a "white" lie?

_____

_____

_____

_____

9. Jesus became angry when he saw merchants selling items for inflated prices in the outer courts of the temple. Describe his actions. How should we deal with our anger? Is it possible to be angry and not sin?

_____

_____

_____

_____

_____

10. Discuss the definition of profanity as "outside the temple." If we defined it today as language "outside the church," how might that change the way we talk?

_____

_____

_____

_____

_____

To Do as Jesus Did

Ephesians 5:1-20

If I had a dollar for every time I've been told to live like Jesus, I'd be massively wealthy right now. This was the basic goal of the WWJD phenomenon twenty-plus years ago that had teenagers wearing plastic bracelets emblazoned with the acronym for "What Would Jesus Do?" If we ask ourselves what Jesus might do in any given situation and seek to emulate his actions, we will indeed live more pure and holy lives. This is essentially what Paul is saying to the Ephesians in the transition from chapter 4 to 5 (let's remember Paul did not write in either chapters or verses).

In chapter 4 Paul cites negative hostilities that must be removed from a believer's life. He mentions anger, malice, bitterness, rage, brawling, and slander. He tells them to substitute forgiveness for each of the aforementioned hostile attitudes. Notice how he skips past revenge and goes straight to forgiveness. The Hebrew Law's eye-for-an-eye statute and the similar retaliation-based tribal mentalities of other Eastern societies bred a culture of seemingly never settled issues. Even Aristotle spoke against bitterness as being unhealthy: "The resentful spirit which refuses reconciliation" (Foulkes, 144). True forgiveness is the weapon of choice for followers of Christ as they interact with the world of negativity on a daily basis.

Forgiveness lived out in spirit or applied verbally is not naturally easy for humans. As Liefeld writes, "Such forgiveness, however, requires more than a good attitude. It requires a deep sense of one's own forgiveness by God and the clear example provided by the sacrifice of Christ" (123). To properly forgive, we must get in touch with our personal forgiveness in and through Christ. If we first feel forgiven, we are in a much better position to provide forgiveness to other people. Liefeld created an equation of sorts to best describe the flow of forgiveness that will lead to a literal lifestyle of embracing and expressing this gift:

> Just as in Christ God forgave us (4:32)
> Be imitators of God . . . as dearly loved children (5:1)
> Just as Christ loved us (5:2)

Holy Living (5:2-8)

WALKING IN LOVE (5:2)

"Christians are different. They are called to 'walk in a manner worthy' of their calling (4:1). That means living differently from others because we *are* different—we have put off the old man and put on the new man. More than that, an ongoing renewal is taking place in us" (Ferguson, 127). The primary outcome of this continuing renewal and refinement process is the ability to live a life of love directed toward other people. To "walk in love" as Paul describes it is at the dynamic center of our identity as people of Jesus Christ. To juxtapose this against Judaism, the crux of a Jew's religious identity was to walk in the Law. This radical difference is but one that distances the new movement from its root in Judaism, but it is certainly the primary one. Clinton Arnold sees love "as the high point and foundation of all Christian ethics" (329). Wiersbe adds, "Since 'God is love' it is logical that God's children will walk in love" (612).

Since living a life bathed in love isn't the natural path for humans, Paul employs a language of sacrifice when speaking on this subject. Christ's *agape* was sacrificial in every regard, and Paul never strays from this underpinning. It is as if he is saying, "If Jesus can live a life of sacrifice that ended with his death on a criminal's cross, we should be able to live and love in a sacrificial manner." There is more than guilt built into this teaching, as it's clear that the only way we can live in such a counterintuitive manner is to view our new lives through the lens of Christ's sacrifice. To love people we do not know is a form of sacrifice. To love people we do not agree with or even respect is an act of sacrifice. To place our lives and interests well behind those of other people is a genuine act of sacrifice. Love quickly loses its mystique and it's level of simple sentimentality when viewed as sacrifice. Actual and effective love is just that, however: a sacrifice modeled on the life of Jesus.

Greek philosophy saw the human life as a compartmentalized sum of its parts. If any one thing were predominant, it would have been reason, which allowed for each compartment to be controlled and mastered. This view gave way to the teaching about the dual natures in humans that Gnostic teachers introduced into the church as a form of doctrine. This aberrant belief taught that two distinctly different natures existed in each person, the physical and spiritual, but only the spiritual nature held importance as the physical nature was already corrupted beyond repair. Obviously this was in direct contradiction to the teachings of Paul, Peter, John, and other early writers. This quickly led to the idea that any sensual excesses could do no further damage due to the total corruption of the physical nature. Paired with the extremely sensually based Greco-Roman cult religions, this view was so pervasive that it was brought into the new church with little pushback. New believers heard that only the spiritual nature was in reach of redemption, and as long as they attended to their spiritual nature the physical nature could be indulged. Paul swam against the proverbial current on this one, so in Ephesians he comes out of the gate with strong words to counter this potentially debilitating philosophy.

In 5:3 he lays out a distinction separating Christians from the sexually and physically indulgent pagans in Ephesus. The false teachers and the cult religion devotees are not only wrong but also dangerous and must be avoided. Patzia writes, "The writer is emphatic in stating that, since his readers are God's holy people, the question is not only one of nonparticipation; rather, there must not be even a hint of these sins among them" (257). It has been suggested that Paul had specific issues regarding sexual sin that prompted him to write both early and often on the subject. It is more likely, though, that his issues were more closely linked to the need to separate from the overt practices of the pagans who seemed to have few, if any, boundaries. Remember that to be *holy* is to be separate and different, which is what Paul is encouraging the Ephesians to emulate.

Sexual impurity and immorality covered wide range of activities that Paul would often cite, in some cases as part of much longer lists of actions to be avoided by believers. Here he adds a specific prohibition against greed, which in this instance is linked to selfish and indulgent sexual activities that can overcome and, in a way, capture an individual.

To Do as Jesus Did

Ephesians 5:4 shifts the purity conversation to the arena of speech and includes prohibitions against obscene speech, foolish words, and coarse humor. Barclay tells us that the ancient Persians believed that to speak about an evil or forbidden act was to introduce it into one's life: "To joke about something or to make it a frequent subject of conversation is to introduce it into the mind and to bring nearer the actual doing of it" (157). This verse would include off-color jokes, sexual innuendo, criticism of other people, and crude language in general. Paul instructs them to replace any and all of the vain and debasing language with thanksgiving to God. An honest question would be this: Is it easier to get rid of all loose, crude, and unnecessary words or to give thanks to God over a considerable portion of the day? The *church* answer is easy, but the real-world reply is much tougher, especially if Paul has a word-for-word swap in mind. For starters, the average person utters approximately 12,000 words per day, which obviously allows for much abuse if this is to be seen as a "negative speech clause." The flip side is also problematic, as the massive word usage would mean each person would be thanking God the majority of the time. Possibly Paul would be fine with the idea of replacing improper, unholy language with uplifting, edifying, positive, kingdom-friendly words, with of course a healthy dose of thanksgiving involved as well.

Ephesians 5:5-10 brings to light a level of immorality that the Greco-Roman world sanctioned and glamorized that was diametrically opposed to the core of Judaism and the teachings of Jesus. The Ephesian church is being asked to stand against the norm of their society and to resist the pull back to their former lives. Paul tells them not to be deceived by the clever orators or impressive teachers they are encountering.

Gnostics actively taught that God refined the spiritual dimension of a person in supernatural ways, but the body represented the physical dimension of the person and was beyond redemption. The caveat of this odd theology was that God only desired to redeem the spiritual element, so any uses of the body would do no further harm as the body was irredeemable. This allowed for an amazing array of immoral behavior and serial practices (many in the name of a cult god or goddess) that Jesus would view as sin. Gnosticism and other cult religious practices led to the teaching of a quasi-gospel within the new church that quickly shifted to a practical aberrant theology.

Paul comes down hard on those who are falling prey to false teachers or societal norms. He instructs steady believers to cease associating with those who pervert the teachings of Christ because God's wrath will be applied to the disobedient. The word for *partner* in Greek holds the connotation of participation with multiple people, so it is much broader than the idea of simply two individuals.

Paul then brings into play the light-versus-darkness motif he so brilliantly weaves into his practical teaching on daily faith living. To Paul the false teachers and pagans are living in a state of oblivious darkness while the believers are now privy to the spectacular light borne of their new faith. The believers have the benefit of the Holy Spirit as their illuminating guide in order to discern the right(eous) path that pleases God. Moule sees verse 8 as foundational to our theology of the Holy Spirit's transformational power: "So had the night of spiritual ignorance and sin penetrated them they were, as it were, night embodied" (131). It is only through the "light" of God's Spirit that believers can truly escape the tyranny of the natural darkness that shrouds this world. The evidence of existing in the light of God's ultimate will is what Paul deems as fruit: goodness, righteousness, and truth.

He builds on the theme of fruit in verses 11-14. The very basic example of fruit would be easy for the Ephesian readers to relate to, as fruit was pivotal to the diet and economy of the era. Simplistically stated, good fruit is a good thing and bad fruit is the extreme opposite. Bad, spoiled fruit is inedible, unhealthy, and has a spoiling effect on other fruit. Good fruit is nutritious, healthy, and, well, yummy. Good fruit meets many needs. Bad fruit is useless. Paul instructs the Ephesians to avoid people who continue to exist in the darkness and produce bad fruit as a result. It's the "one bad apple" analogy that if you exist too closely to bad fruit, you too may begin to spoil. He emphasizes this point by telling his readers not only to avoid evildoers but also to expose them. Hughes writes, "The effects of darkness and light are antithetical. Darkness shelters evil and helps it fester, so that 'it is shameful even to mention what the disobedient do in secret' (v. 12). Night has no shame" (166). To expose evil to the light of Christ is to shine a beam of reality into the disguise of arrogance and self-focus that shrouds it. Evil and sin are only enticing when they lurk in the shadows of darkness. Exposed to the light of righteousness, each is seen for what it actually is.

In verses 15-20 Paul shifts to a form of wisdom-based teaching similar to that found in Ecclesiastes and Proverbs. Paul's view that Jesus will return soon is evident in his writings as he stresses a hurriedness both to know and to do God's will in life. The days are not only short but also "evil," leading Paul to urge caution in the day-to-day decisions of life. His focus is on making wise choices prompted by the Holy Spirit and seeing each day as an opportunity to impact the kingdom of God positively. In order to live wisely, it is paramount to seek to God's will for one's life. Since there are two arenas of God's will, the general and specific, the believer must seek to know what all Christians should do for the kingdom and the exact and specific role God has planned uniquely for them. There are duties and roles that all believers share and pointedly specific things God calls each individual to do.

Within the context of "wise" living in the "evil" world of the mid-first century, Paul instructs the Ephesians to "not get drunk with wine, which is debauchery, but be filled with the Spirit" (v. 18). Drinking wine to excess was common in most pagan Greco-Roman religions, so Paul is likely drawing a line of distinction between the sensual and indulgent cult celebrations and the worship of those who follow Jesus. Jews would not have needed this instruction, but Paul was the evangelist to the Gentiles, most of whom would have been familiar with the combination of religious ritual and the abundant consumption of wine.

One cult in particular had elevated the wine issue in Ephesus: "Wine and drunkenness were central features of the worship of Dionysus (also known as Bacchus). In the frenzied and ecstatic Dionysiac rituals, intoxication with wine was tantamount to being filled with the spirit of Dionysus" (Arnold, 33). If former Dionysian followers brought even a fraction of this practice into the church and saw wine as a path to being filled with the Spirit of God, bad theology would lead to bad practice in short order. Paul chooses to erase the potential issue with this prohibition against becoming intoxicated with wine. He doesn't say to abstain from drinking wine, which some denominations have extrapolated from this single verse; rather he says do not drink wine to excess. A sidebar theological truth is this: there is only one path to being filled with the Holy Spirit, and that is through seeking a stronger presence through personal spiritual practices.

Continuing with the theme of worship and personal spirituality, Paul instructs his readers to interact with fellow believers in a spirit of praise and thanksgiving. Arnold tells us, "The three terms Paul chooses here—*psalmos, hymnos* and *ode*—stress the variety of forms of music in the early church" (34). This praiseful attitude and lifestyle would certainly stand out and elicit notice of the unusual attitudes of the Christians in Ephesus. It would also personify the developing reality of Christian community among the believers there who were seeking to live in genuine *agape*. To place the needs of others in front of one's own is the definition of *agape* love and is the only lasting way to "submit to one another out of reverence for Christ" (v. 21).

This verse is the beginning of a complete section on mutual submission that would set Christianity apart from Judaism and all other religions of the Greco-Roman world. To willfully submit to another person out of reverence for Christ is a teaching that over time would literally alter the course of humanity. Despite being patently anti-Greek and anti-Roman, it would outlive the former's influence and the latter's reign.

Life Lessons

In the previous session, Paul highlighted the negatives of the average pagan Gentile lifestyle. It was a "Do Not" list of behaviors and actions for the Christian Gentiles to resist as they lived into their new lives. In this session we see Paul tacking to the positive by laying out the virtues and practices believers must follow if they honor God with their lives and positively influence the world. Followers of Jesus must be people of true love and empathy in the midst of gross animosity, hatred, and bigotry. *Agape* love is the root and genesis of all ethical behaviors and must underpin the actions Paul commands in this section. To "walk in love" as Paul teaches is at the dynamic center of our identity as people of Christ. From this walk, or lifestyle as we might better understand the concept, will flow forgiveness, holiness, purity, and thankful spirits. This "odd" way of embracing life and the world can't help but highlight a difference from the mass of people slogging through a life mired in the natural negatives of daily, unredeemed living. One doesn't have to go to Haiti or Africa to have a serious impact for Christ. One needs only to leave their front door daily with the intention of living out an *agape* life that is so counter to the norm that people will take notice. Over time, the differences will shed light on the reality of Jesus and open doors for us to share our faith.

1. Do you believe that to truly forgive another person you must first forgive yourself? Put another way, do you believe that in order to provide forgiveness, you must first know what it's like to be forgiven? Comment on your response.

_____

_____

_____

_____

_____

2. How does Paul tie love and sacrifice together?

_____

_____

_____

_____

_____

3. Sensual excesses were part of some cult religions and were seen as a form of intimacy with the god or goddess being worshiped. Paul taught that such sin must not be part of a believer's life, much less part of religious ceremony. Do you think this is why we tend to view sexual sin as worse than other sins today?

_____

_____

_____

_____

_____

4. Another difference the Christian was to embody had to do with speech habits. Paul taught the Ephesians to erase all coarse humor, foolish words, and obscene language. How might this teaching change our speech habits today?

_____

_____

_____

_____

_____

5. Describe and explain the Gnostic doctrine of the dual person.

_____

_____

_____

_____

_____

6. In what ways is today's world continuing to live in the darkness Paul described?

_____

_____

_____

_____

_____

7. List the fruit of darkness and the fruit of the light. Describe how bad, spoiled fruit can be bad for one's body, and then take it a step further and describe how bad fruit can be unhealthy for the body of Christ.

_____

_____

_____

_____

_____

8. If Scripture never states that it is sinful to drink alcohol, why do so many denominations continue to assign abstinence to the Bible? What is Paul's main problem with wine in the Ephesian letter?

_____

_____

_____

_____

_____

9. Why is it important for Christians to present a worshipful, praiseful, and positive countenance to other people? How are we doing this?

_____

_____

_____

_____

_____

10. Submission, weakness, and meekness are words often linked together. Jesus, however, was described as meek in the sense of "power under control." How would his take on meekness change our views on submitting to one another and being vulnerable like Jesus?

_____

_____

_____

_____

_____

The Laundry List
Ephesians 5:22–6:20

The Household Codes

Paul often ends his letters with a laundry list of sorts, covering many topics as he winds down. The final chapter of the Ephesian letter is no exception. Beginning in 5:22 he kicks off with a series of instructions commonly referred to as the Household Codes. Ancient Greek writers like Plato and Aristotle wrote in copious detail on household management issues, as the family unit and the home were foundational to the stability of both Greek and Roman society. It is important to note that Paul did not originate the idea of a code for family living; he simply "Christianized" the existing codes already in place. Fowl writes,

> To the extent to which Christians found themselves in conventionally structured patriarchal households, Ephesians gives them guidance about how best to live in those households as followers of Christ. The most important thing Paul offers the Ephesians is the example of seeing and interpreting the world through Christologically ground lenses rather than lenses ground by Greco-Roman social custom and convention. Developing this specific habit must lie at the basis of all attempts to walk worthily. (15)

Paul's exhortations to walk worthily of one's new calling in Christ can also be described in terms of submission. Modern readers may view submission in a negative light, but so too would the original recipients, first-century males, who held naturally privileged positions in the Greco-Roman society. Ferguson aptly explains it this way: "In the opening three chapters Paul has for all practical purposes been expounding what it means for us to be in Christ" (144).

The Submissive Wife (5:22)

Since Paul was not likely married at the time of this writing, he could get away with beginning his teaching session on marriage with the wife and female. In today's much more equal world of the West, some might question why he chose to begin with the woman. The answer would lie in the intense patriarchal-hierarchal family and societal structure of his day.

Paul is careful not to bring unneeded scrutiny upon the church while teaching the equalizing work of Christ (Gal 3:23). Ephesian believers lived within the Roman *pater familias,* or rule of the father, which placed specific role restrictions on the wife/mother. If, say, Paul stated that wives were equal in Christ (which they obviously were) and thus they should also be equal within the family and societal structure, it's possible a version of anarchy would have taken place. Any noticeable change in how women functioned in the strictly ordered society would have cast a negative light on the institution of the Christian church. Fowl suggests that Paul pushed for the Ephesians and Colossians to order their households in conventional ways in order to show that they were not a threat to the political order, which would subsequently also allow them to engage more effectively in sharing their new faith (42).

The Interpreter's Commentary says that "loyal obedience is required but not servile capitulation" (843) on behalf of the female spouse. The commentary writers go on to say that Paul has in mind "the principle of reciprocal responsibility" (843), which would also cover interpersonal relationships of all types. Since there is no verb form of *submit* in verse 22, we must see this as a continuation of the preceding verse centering on mutual submission. Ferguson suggests a more literal translation: "Submitting to one another in reverence/fear of Christ . . . the wives to their own husbands in the Lord" (148). He goes on to wrap up the issue this way: "The calling is to submission. Paul's counsel to the wife is focused exclusively on her marriage relationship to her husband. There is a primary and absolute submission that is to the Lord Jesus Christ. Here, in talking to believers, Paul urges wives to express that in their disposition towards and relationship with their husbands" (149).

The Submissive Husband (5:25-33)

"The wife has been told to submit to her husband because of the God-given role of leadership and authority given to him" (Ferguson, 150). This rationale is often explained by citing the order of creation with the rib used in the Genesis 1 account being the *source* of woman. This certainly speaks to a hierarchal structure that naturally, even permanently, places the woman below the man. Obviously this is a contentious view that is challenged by the "equality" verses found elsewhere in Paul's writings. Another option is the lordship doctrine where Jesus is first, man is second, and the woman is third—and all of life must be seen through this particular lens. The most fundamental of religious groups might hold to this strict and ordered view, but credible biblical commentators like Sinclair Ferguson, Gordon Fee, and R. Kent Hughes opt for a simpler, more spiritual meaning of "He (the husband) is head of his wife not because she was created out of Adam's rib (source) but because God has constituted the relationship in this way, for his own purposes" (Ferguson, 150).

The creation stories of Genesis show that male and female were to be one flesh, so a vertical ordering would be an abrogation of earlier Scripture. Paul teaches the man, the husband, to model his love for his wife after that of Jesus to the church. This would be a form of *agape* love that is based on submission and on placing the needs and welfare of his wife ahead of his own. It can tip to the level of confusion when Paul adds the many ways Jesus loves the church and instructs that husbands must follow suit. If, however, the Genesis meshing of husband and wife into one joint entity remains in the forefront, the entire teaching makes great sense. If husband and wife are one body and one flesh, then it would be problematic for him to hate himself. To love your wife as you love yourself based on Christ's love for the church (of which we are all part) seems both natural and healthy. As Ferguson states, "The Gospel itself is thus a manual for husbands, training them how to love their wives" (154).

Children and Parents (6:1-4)

The opening verses of chapter 6 are the favorite of many parents. These are the verses parents ask their children to learn by memory. It is obvious that Paul is focusing on the entire family unit in his continuing teaching on the household codes as he shifts from husband and wife to parent/child relationships. Earlier Paul used "obey" in the voluntary sense, but here he is quite emphatic and firm with the command simply to obey parents because it is the right thing to do. There's no wiggle room involved, no outs by invoking the "lousy parent" clause. Christian families will be defined in part by the respect and obedience of the children to their parents.

Due to the Roman *pater familias* that saw the father as the supreme ruler of the family, it was understood that children were to obey their parents or face stiff consequences. O'Brien believes that Gentile pagans of that era were dealing with a rise in disobedience among their children. Christian children were instructed to model a distinctly different attitude toward their parents for uniquely different reasons. They were to obey and honor their parents based on a love for Christ that would naturally flow into the parent-child relationship. The classic Roman child would obey out of abject fear rather than actual love. The Roman father held the powers of expulsion from the family, severe punishments, degradation of status, and, in some cases, even death. An "obey or pay dearly" mentality was in place. Paul seeks to replace the inherent motivation for disobedience to parents with submissive love, much as does did in reshaping the husband/wife relationship earlier. It is important to note that this is the only command in the Household Codes that comes with a promise, in this case a long life.

Paul also ups the ante for the Christian father with the admonition not to provoke or anger his children. This one sentence seems to lessen the *pater familias,* or at least spiritualize it by seeking some level of mutual respect and honor. Paul's message is to be careful not to provoke children to anger in the process of being intentional in training and instructing them in the teachings of Jesus. This command does not lessen the authority of the parent or lighten the amount of parenting that will otherwise occur. It does, however, change the intent of the parenting. Bruce writes, "Fathers (or parents) are urged not to assert their authority over children in a manner more calculated to provoke resentment than ready obedience" (398). If the new intent is to parent children using the example of Jesus, the resulting obedience would stem from the heart rather than the mind filled with fear. If the parents are also learning along the way and striving to live like Christ as they continue to mature, the children will see that their personal progress and maturation is a never-ending process.

Slaves Are Still Slaves (6:5-9)

Hughes wrote, "It has been estimated that there were some 60,000,000 slaves in the Roman Empire, and that as many as one-third of the populations of large cities such as Rome, Corinth and Ephesus were slaves" (205). Obviously slavery was a way of life in the Greco-Roman world of the mid-first century. This urges a question as to why Paul did not use this opportunity to command new believers to free their slaves as a result of their new faith lives. This has been a particularly vexing problem for the church for two millennia. The easiest answer to why Paul (and Jesus) did not work to abolish slavery is tied to the enormous social and economic upheaval caused by a portion of the population breaking away from the norm and freeing their slaves. Roman leaders would not have looked on this with any degree of favor, and Paul seemed to be keenly aware of the tenuous relationship between Caesar and the new movement. It is important to note the staggering number of slaves in question within the Roman Empire at the time of Paul's writing. Bradley affirms Hughes: "Over one-third of the population of Rome in the first century was slaves. The servile proportion of the population of Italy in the time of Augustus can be fairly estimated at 35 per cent, a figure comparable to that for Brazil in 1800 and for the United States in 1820" (12).

Another point to consider is that first-century slaves held more rights and options than slaves in the New World. Hughes reports that "50% of slaves were freed by the age of thirty and even while in slavery they could own property—including other slaves!" (206). He goes on to say that the new church would be seen as economically subversive if it required the freeing of slaves (206). While this rationale doesn't fully lighten the sting of prolonging such a patently non-Christian institution, it does shed light on the immensity of the dilemma Paul faced.

Dear Slaves (6:5-8)

Biblical patriarchs Abraham, Isaac, and Jacob were slave owners, and, as already noted, a sizeable percentage of the Greco-Roman population was indentured slaves. To his credit, Paul never seeks to justify the practice of slavery; he simply acknowledges its reality and offers instruction designed to assist Christian slaves and owners in living as people of faith within this unjust social structure. He begins his teaching by instructing the slaves to obey their human masters with the type of respect and honor they hold for Christ. This had to be a "Wait, what?" moment for the large number of slaves who had accepted Jesus as Lord. Paul straightaway elevates the difficulty factor by adding "in the sincerity of your hearts," which is a kind way of telling the slaves to honor their masters "and really mean it"!

Paul is teaching a form of *agape* where the follower of Christ becomes subservient as a lifestyle. This may appear an easier feat for a slave who is already in a veritable caste system than for a free person. It would not have been, however, if the second admonition were also followed. To accept one's position as a slave without "succumbing to guile, scheming, deceit, or any kind of base nature" (Arnold, 423) would be closer to genuine *agape* than most free believers ever reach.

Verse 6 speaks of the next bit of heavy lifting for the slave: "Not serving to be seen, as people pleasers, but as slaves of Christ doing the will of God from the heart." This is yet another counterintuitive tenet of Christianity. The natural human reaction is to please people, especially those with power and position. Most people are also taught that honest, hard work will pay off with certain rewards. Paul is teaching slaves that they should work hard and be excellent slaves not for the master but for Christ. There may not be a real-time, tangible reward for the hard, honest work, but that must no longer be the objective. Paul could have in mind an abundance of spiritual fruit—the blessings of peace, purpose, and direction. He coins a new phrase with "not serving to be seen," and in doing so further develops the doctrine of "higher calling." Arnold applies it this way: "Such superficially motivated service is tantamount to being a 'people-pleaser,' but believers have a higher calling than that" (423). Ferguson thinks Paul had an ulterior motive in these teachings, since slaves could model their new lives as a way of positively influencing their owners:

> The earthly master who is not a believer cannot understand why the Christian slave is so responsive, so gracious, so diligent. Obedience to the master is not *by way of eye-service, as people-pleasers* (verse 6). It is always an expression of obedience to Christ, (so) the slave's good will to his master is an expression of his love for his Lord. (169)

OWNERS STILL OWN (6:9)

Paul shifts to the slave owners for his next round of instruction. There is little doubt that with one-third of the population being enslaved, the entire society lived, as Ferguson describes it, in a "zone of conflict" (173). The potential for a constant climate of friction and acrimony was ever present, and Paul instructed both slaves and masters to keep the issues to a minimum by living out their new faith while remaining in their respective stations. The social construct was not changing, so the players in this cultural drama were asked to work within the unbalanced framework to bring small, slow, incremental change. Wiersbe writes, "Servants are still servants when they trust Christ, and masters are still masters. Rather, the Christian faith brings harmony by working in the heart. God gives us new motivation, not a new organization" (621).

Paul tells the slave owners to view the welfare of their slaves in a new, more humane way. Slaves are to work harder and owners are to be fair and honest toward them. The owners must also cease using the enormous power provided them by the Roman government to oppress their slaves. Owners held the right to put slaves to death if they rebelled or took part in insurrection. The standard approach to keeping order and increasing productivity was through the threat of punishment. Paul speaks in a counterintuitive manner that could be construed as being revolutionary for his era. He urges owners to model Christ in the entire scope of their relationships with slaves, keeping in mind that they too have a Master. To paraphrase William Barclay, the Christian master who owns servants is also a servant with a master. It is this mindset and model that must be pervasive within this flawed social system (209).

The Reality of Evil (6:10-20)

Paul sees the entire cosmos as a conflict zone where a supernatural battle is taking place between the forces of good and evil. This sounds like a line from a science-fiction movie trailer, but it is an apt description of Paul's theology of the reality of evil. His seeming intent here is to assist the Ephesians to be on guard against the rampant onslaught of evil that will soon come upon the movement. He utilizes imagery from Isaiah that depicts the armor of God, in effect "the Lord of Hosts as a warrior dressed for battle as he goes forth to vindicate his people" (O'Brien, 457). Obviously this is highly metaphorical, but nonetheless effective, as he stresses the abject reality of a cosmic battle between God and Satan. The Ephesians are to find solace in the foreknowledge that God will win in the end, but until that future, fateful day, they will be engaged in the battle.

What does this metaphorical armor look like? The Ephesians would have noticed straightaway that the armor described by Paul did not match the contemporary Roman armor. The ones Paul mentions are quite dated. This getup is much more garden-variety Old Testament than Greco-Roman, but the takeaway for the original readers and consequently for today's readers is simply this: *The power and strength one is given as a gift from God is the real armor and weaponry needed to do battle with supernatural evil.* Liefeld explains,

> The source of strength is the Lord Himself, and in particular the *mighty power* just referred to (v.10). The means are the various pieces of armor, not only as separate parts but as a whole, *the full armor* (v.11). While this phrase represents a single Greek word, *panoplia,* that word is itself a compound of two words: all or whole and tool or weapon. Its common meaning is "the full equipment of the heavily armored foot-soldier." The English term is derived from this, *panoply,* and can refer to full protective covering, ceremonial dress or a complete display of something in all its parts. In this case the emphasis seems to be not so much on being in full military dress or having every weapon, as on having total protection, with enough of the individual pieces identified to show the need of God's full provision for the spiritual battle. (Liefeld, 157)

Paul urges his readers to arm themselves spiritually because the days will grow even more evil. It's also easy to see in Paul's letters his belief that the world has a short shelf life. His writings are filled with a sense of real urgency based on his belief that Jesus would soon return. To Paul, not being busy doing the work of the kingdom is sinful and selfish. The Ephesians are to "suit up for battle," but to do so with haste as they will soon face the twin needs of resisting evil and intentionally progressing God's kingdom.

Praying toward Prayer (6:18-20)

It would be difficult to prioritize the "armor" of God or the spiritual disciplines Paul describes, but if forced to do so, prayer would be at or near the top of the list. The ongoing spiritual war between the forces of good and evil includes each and every believer. There is not an out for conscientious objectors. We are soldiers whether we like it or not. Our main weapon must be that of prayer, which Paul places after all other pieces of armor are described. Thus prayer completes the outfit of the spiritual soldier. He regularly tells us to "pray without ceasing," which could mean to live in continual communication mode with God. Here he fleshes this out with the words, "pray in the Spirit at all times (on all occasions) with all kinds of prayers and requests" (v. 18a). Continuing with the military theme, soldiers are soldiers day in and day out and do not cease to be soldiers while on leave or inactive duty. It is the same for Christians. Christians are "on" constantly and forever, and thus our primary lifeline to God is prayer, which is to be done at all times.

There is also a community element in place. In verse 18b Paul tells us to "always pray for the saints." Who are the saints? *Saint* is a biblical word for set-apart, holy believers in Jesus Christ. This means we are to regularly pray for our fellow believers, which is a poetically beautiful thing its own right but is also quite practical in that it will keep us from experiencing a litany of self-focused prayers.

Life Lessons

To a large degree, Paul's rendering of the Household Codes was an attempt to "Christianize" the order and flow of familial relationships for the Ephesian believers. The Greco-Roman culture gave the father complete control over the family. The gospel Paul proclaimed provided unprecedented equality for all people, but it had to be implemented slowly and with deftness so that no form of social anarchy broke out. The wife would be equal and would have a defined role but would allow the man/husband to be the spiritual leader of the family. The husband was to love his wife with a love first modeled by Christ, and would lead the family with a servant's heart. Children would be treated with more respect, and fear would cease being a parenting technique. That said, children would obey their parents because it was seen as an act of faith.

The thorniest of the codes to be followed centered on slavery. Since this is not a church issue for many local congregations in the West, today's questions tend to focus on why Paul did not seek the abolition of such an inhumane practice. Slavery is, however, a continuing blight upon the world, and as Christians we should actively seek the abolition of slavery, human trafficking, and the plight of forced refugees regardless of what Paul taught.

Our takeaway from Paul's final words to the Ephesian church is simple: regard evil as being very real, very dangerous, and in direct contrast to all we hold as holy and right. To resist and fight evil is to be active as a follower of Christ. Paul's ending with prayer seems appropriate; it is our connection to power and wisdom. Through prayer we can be and do more, which is what our goal must be. Paul's words were sound advice then, and they are sound advice today.

1. How do you make peace with the fact that neither Paul nor other New Testament writers advocated for the abolition of slavery?

_____

_____

_____

_____

_____

2. In your opinion, which party had the biggest challenge living out Paul's teaching: slaves or slave owners? Explain your answer.

_____

_____

_____

_____

_____

3. Does Paul's new phrase to Christian slaves, "not serving to be seen," have modern application as well?

_____

_____

_____

_____

_____

4. Do you personally view Satan or the devil as a person or as a system of evil? Explain your views.

_____

_____

_____

_____

_____

5. Do you believe that Satan is as powerful today as he/it was in the first century? If so, describe ways today's believers can protect themselves from evil influences.

_____

_____

_____

_____

_____

6. Explain what it means to be "living in continuous prayer," and cite examples.

_____

_____

_____

_____

_____

7. If God already knows what is going to happen, why should we pray continuously and why should we pray for one another? List possible benefits of such dedicated prayer.

_____

_____

_____

_____

_____

8. How do you explain Paul's teaching that wives must submit to their husbands in everything in light of his words in Galatians 3:26-29?

_____

_____

_____

_____

_____

9. Paul's instructions on parent-child relationships were unique for that era. If children honored and obeyed their parents "in the Lord," they were promised a long and good life. Did he have actual years in mind? Explain your views.

_____

_____

_____

_____

_____

Works Cited

Arnold, Clinton E. *Illustrated Bible Backgrounds Commentary.* Grand Rapids MI: Zondervan, 2002.

———. *Exegetical Commentary on the New Testament—Ephesians.* Grand Rapids MI: Zondervan, 2010.

Barclay, William. *Letters to the Galatians & Ephesians.* Louisville KY: WJK Press, revised 2002.

Bradley, Keith. *Slavery and Society at Rome: Key Themes in Ancient History.* Cambridge, UK: Cambridge University Press, 1994.

Bickel, Bruce, and Stan Janiz. *Finding your Identity in Christ.* Eugene OR: Harvest House, 1996.

Bruce, F. F. *Epistles to the Colossians, to Philemon, and to the Ephesians.* Grand Rapids: W. B. Eerdmans, 1984.

Buechner, Frederick. *Wishful Thinking: A Theological ABC.* New York: Harper & Row, 1973.

Carver, William O. *The Glory of God in the Christian Calling: A Study of Ephesian Epistle.* Nashville: Broadman Press, 1949.

Ferguson, Sinclair B. *Let's Study Ephesians.* Edinburgh, UK: The Banner of Truth Trust, 2005.

Foulkes, Francis. *Ephesians.* Tyndale N.T. Commentaries. Leicester, UK/Grand Rapids MI: IVP, 1989.

Howell, David B. *Ephesians: God Calls a New People.* Macon GA: Smyth & Helwys, 1996.

Hughes, R. Kent. *Ephesians: The Mystery of the Body of Christ.* Weaton IL: Crossway Books, 1990.

Layman, Charles M., editor. *The Interpreter's One-Volume Commentary on the Bible.* Nashville: Abingdon, 1971.

Liefeld, Walter L. *Ephesians.* Downers Grove IL: IVP Press, 1997.

Motyer, Stephen. *Ephesians: Free to be One.* Grand Rapids MI: Baker, 1994.

O'Brien, Peter T. *The Letter to the Ephesians.* Cambridge, UK: Eerdmans Publishing, 1999.

Patzia, Arthur G. *Ephesians, Colossians, Philemon.* New International Biblical Commentary. Carlisle, UK: Paternoster Press, 1995.

Phillips, J. B. *Your God Is Too Small.* New York: Macmillan, 1967.

Phillips, John. *Exploring Ephesians & Philippians.* Grand Rapids MI: Kregel, 1993.

Snodgrass, Klyne. *NIV Application Commentary on Ephesians.* Grand Rapids MI: Zondervan, 1996.

Steadman, Ray, C. *Our Riches in Christ.* Grand Rapids MI: Discovery House Publishing, 1998.

Stott, John R.W. *Message of Ephesians.* Leicester, UK: IVP, 1979.

Thurston, Bonnie. *Reading Colossians, Ephesians & 2 Thessalonians.* New York: Crossroads, 1995.

Wiersbe, Warren W., and David B. Howell. *The Wiersbe Bible Commentary.* Colorado Springs: David C Cook, 2007.

Young, Brad H. *Paul The Jewish Theologian; A Pharisee Among Christians, Jews & Gentiles.* Peabody MA: Henrickson Publications, 1997.

Study the Bible ...

Series

a book at a time

Series Editor:
Michael D. McCullar

The *Sessions* Series is our expanding set of Bible studies designed to encourage a deeper encounter with Scripture. Each volume includes eight to ten lessons as well as resource pages to facilitate preparation, class discussion, or individual Bible study.

**Sessions
with Genesis**
The Story Begins
by Tony W. Cartledge

**Sessions
with Samuel**
Stories from the Edge
by Tony W. Cartledge

**Sessions
with Psalms**
Prayers for All Seasons
by Eric and Alicia D. Porterfield

**Sessions
with Matthew**
Becoming a Family of Faith
by William D. Shiell

**Sessions
with Mark**
Following Jesus at Full Speed
*by Michael D. McCullar &
Rickey Letson*

**Sessions
with Luke**
Following Jesus on the Journey
to Christian Character
by Timothy W. Brock

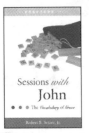